Philip Schaff

A Christian Catechism for Sunday-Schools and Families

In Fifty-Two Lessons, with Proof-Texts and Notes

Philip Schaff

A Christian Catechism for Sunday-Schools and Families
In Fifty-Two Lessons, with Proof-Texts and Notes

ISBN/EAN: 9783744755368

Printed in Europe, USA, Canada, Australia, Japan

Cover: Foto ©Lupo / pixelio.de

More available books at **www.hansebooks.com**

A
CHRISTIAN CATECHISM

FOR

SUNDAY-SCHOOLS AND FAMILIES.

IN FIFTY-TWO LESSONS.

WITH PROOF-TEXTS AND NOTES.

BY

PHILIP SCHAFF, D.D.,

Professor in the Union Theological Seminary, New York.

FROM HOME TO THE SCHOOL: FROM THE SCHOOL TO THE CHURCH:
FROM THE CHURCH TO HEAVEN.

NEW EDITION.

PHILADELPHIA:
AMERICAN SUNDAY-SCHOOL UNION,
No. 1122 CHESTNUT STREET.

NEW YORK: NOS. 8 AND 10 BIBLE HOUSE, ASTOR PLACE.

Entered according to Act of Congress, in the year 1880, by the
AMERICAN SUNDAY-SCHOOL UNION,
In the Office of the Librarian of Congress, at Washington.

PREFACE.

BY THE EDITOR.

THIS Catechism was originally prepared for family use, and has been highly valued by pastors, families, and Sunday-school teachers in different denominations.

Dr. Schaff has generously presented the plates and copyright of this work (large and small edition) to the American Sunday-School Union, and revised and adapted it to its use.

"A catechism on the Christian religion should present the articles of faith fresh from the fountain of the word of God to the mind and heart of the pupil for his instruction and comfort in life and in death. It should move in the central current of Christian truth. The more important denominational differences may be stated for historical information, but in a kind and charitable spirit, and with a view to promote, rather than to diminish, unity and harmony among the various branches of the kingdom of Christ."

In the present work the author has happily combined the above advantages of an historical with those of a doctrinal catechism, and clearness and simplicity of style with comprehensiveness of doctrine. His arrangement in commencing with the Lord's Prayer follows the common educational order, for children are usually first taught the Lord's Prayer, or how to pray; after this the Apostles' Creed, or what to believe; and the Ten Commandments, or how to act. The subjects are naturally divided into fifty-two lessons, corresponding to the number of Lord's Days in a year. The Scripture passages marked by an asterisk (*) are to be committed to memory as a treasury of proof-texts on Christian doctrine and life. In this improved form the book is heartily commended to pastors, parents, teachers, and pupils who feel the need of a simple yet complete Biblical Union Catechism to aid in preserving the form of sound doctrine and the purity of Christian life.*

May it be owned and blessed even more abundantly in the future by Him who said, "Suffer the little children to come unto me, and forbid them not; for of such is the kingdom of God."

EDWIN W. RICE.

PHILADELPHIA, 1880.

* A cheaper edition of this Catechism is issued by the American Sunday-school Union, without the proof-texts and notes.

TABLE OF LESSONS.

THE LORD'S PRAYER.—THE CREED.—THE TEN COMMANDMENTS.   Pages 5–8.

INTRODUCTORY LESSONS.

                                                                  PAGE

I.—The True End of Man 9
II.—The Way of Salvation 11
III.—The Holy Scriptures 12
IV.—The Old and the New Testament 16
V.—The Old Testament 19
VI.—The New Testament 20

PART FIRST.

THE LORD'S PRAYER.

VII.—Of Prayer 23
VIII.—The Lord's Prayer 28
IX.—The Address 29
X.—The First Three Petitions 31
XI.—The Last Three Petitions 35

PART SECOND.

THE APOSTLES' CREED, OR, THE CHRISTIAN FAITH.

XII.—Of the Christian Faith 40
XIII.—The Apostles' Creed 43
XIV.—The Existence and Attributes of God 45
XV.—The Unity and Trinity of God 47

TABLE OF LESSONS.

	PAGE
XVI.—The Creation of the World	49
XVII.—Preservation and Providence	51
XVIII.—The State of Innocence	53
XIX.—The Fall	56
XX.—Sin	60
XXI.—The Punishment of Sin	63
XXII.—Preparation for the Coming of Christ	66
XXIII.—Jesus Christ.—His Names	70
XXIV.—The Person of Christ	72
XXV.—The Two States of Christ	76
XXVI.—The Birth and Childhood of Christ	77
XXVII.—The Public Life and Ministry of Christ	79
XXVIII.—The Passion and Death of Christ	83
XXIX.—The Burial, and Descent into Hades	86
XXX.—The Resurrection, and Ascension of Christ	88
XXXI.—The Sitting at the Right Hand of God, and Return to Judgment	90
XXXII.—The Threefold Office and Work of Christ	93
XXXIII.—The Holy Spirit	95
XXXIV.—The Christian Church, and the Communion of Saints	99
XXXV.—The Means of Grace	104
XXXVI.—Holy Baptism	108
XXXVII.—The Lord's Supper	111
XXXVIII.—The Order of Salvation.—Regeneration	115
XXXIX.—Justification and Sanctification	121
XL.—The Resurrection of the Body, and the Life Everlasting	125

PART THIRD.

THE TEN COMMANDMENTS, OR, THE CHRISTIAN LIFE.

XLI.—The Ten Commandments	130
XLII.—The First Commandment	133
XLIII.—The Second Commandment	136

TABLE OF LESSONS.

	PAGE
XLIV.—The Third Commandment	140
XLV.—The Fourth Commandment	142
XLVI.—The Fifth Commandment	146
XLVII.—The Sixth Commandment	150
XLVIII.—The Seventh Commandment	154
XLIX.—The Eighth Commandment	156
L.—The Ninth Commandment	159
LI.—The Tenth Commandment	162
LII.—Concluding Questions	166

THE LORD'S PRAYER.

Our Father who art in heaven:

Hallowed be thy name. Thy kingdom come. Thy will be done in earth as *it is* in heaven. Give us this day our daily bread. And forgive us our debts, as we forgive our debtors. And lead us not into temptation, but deliver us from evil.

For thine is the kingdom, and the power, and the glory, forever. Amen.

THE CREED.

I believe in God the Father Almighty, Maker of heaven and earth.

And in Jesus Christ his only begotten Son our Lord; who was conceived by the Holy Ghost, born of the Virgin Mary; suffered under Pontius Pilate, was crucified, dead, and buried; He descended into hades;* the third day He rose from the dead; He ascended into heaven; and sitteth at the right hand of God the Father Almighty; from thence He shall come to judge the quick and the dead.

* The place of departed spirits.

I believe in the Holy Ghost; the holy catholic Church, the communion of saints; the forgiveness of sins; the resurrection of the body, and the life everlasting. Amen.

THE TEN COMMANDMENTS.

God spake all these words, saying:

I *am* the Lord thy God, which have brought thee out of the land of Egypt, out of the house of bondage.

I. Thou shalt have no other gods before Me.

II. Thou shalt not make unto thee any graven image, or any likeness *of any thing* that *is* in heaven above, or that *is* in the earth beneath, or that *is* in the water under the earth: thou shalt not bow down thyself to them, nor serve them.

For I the Lord thy God *am* a jealous God, visiting the iniquity of the fathers upon the children unto the third and fourth *generation* of them that hate Me; and shewing mercy unto thousands of them that love Me, and keep My commandments.

III. Thou shalt not take the name of the Lord thy God in vain.

For the Lord will not hold him guiltless that taketh His name in vain.

IV. Remember the sabbath day, to keep it holy. Six days shalt thou labor, and do all thy work: but the seventh day *is* the sabbath of the Lord thy God: *in it* thou shalt not do any work, thou, nor thy son, nor thy daughter, thy manservant, nor thy maidservant, nor thy cattle, nor thy stranger that *is* within thy gates.

For *in* six days the Lord made heaven and earth, the sea, and all that in them *is*, and rested the seventh day: wherefore the Lord blessed the sabbath day, and hallowed it.

V. Honor thy father and thy mother: that thy days may be long upon the land which the Lord thy God giveth thee.

VI. Thou shalt not kill.

VII. Thou shalt not commit adultery.

VIII. Thou shalt not steal.

IX. Thou shalt not bear false witness against thy neighbor.

X. Thou shalt not covet thy neighbor's house, thou shalt not covet thy neighbor's wife, nor his manservant, nor his maidservant, nor his ox, nor his ass, nor any thing that *is* thy neighbor's.

Thou shalt love the Lord thy God with all thy heart, and with all thy soul, and with all thy mind. This is the first and great commandment.

And the second *is* like unto it: Thou shalt love thy neighbor as thyself.

On these two commandments hang all the law and the prophets.

A CHRISTIAN CATECHISM.

INTRODUCTORY LESSONS.

I. The True End of Man.

1. *Who made you?*

Almighty God, our heavenly Father.

* Gen. 1, 27. God created man in his own image, in the image of God created he him.

Ps. 100, 3. It is he [God] that hath made us, and not we ourselves; we are his people, and the sheep of his pasture.

Job 33, 4. The Spirit of God hath made me, and the breath of the Almighty hath given me life.

Mal. 2, 10. Have we not all one Father? Hath not one God created us?

Ps. 33, 6; 119, 73; Job 10, 8; Neh. 9, 6; John 1, 3; Col. 1, 16.

2. *Who redeemed you?*

Our Lord Jesus Christ.

* 1 Pet. 1, 18. 19. Ye were not redeemed with corruptible things, as silver and gold, ... but with the precious blood of Christ.

1 Cor. 6, 20. Ye are bought with a price: therefore glorify God in your body and in your spirit, which are God's.

1 Tim. 2, 6; Tit. 2, 14; Acts 20, 28; Heb. 9, 14; 1 John 1, 7; Rev. 1, 5.

3. *Who sanctifies you?*

The Holy Spirit.

* 1 Cor. 6, 11. Ye are washed, ye are sanctified, ye are justified in the name of the Lord Jesus, and by the Spirit of our God.

1 Pet. 1, 2. Elect according to the foreknowledge of God

the Father, through sanctification of the Spirit, unto obedience and sprinkling of the blood of Jesus Christ.
Heb. 10, 22; 2 Thess. 2, 13.

4. *For what end were you created?*

For the glory of God and for eternal blessedness.

* Rom. 11, 36. Of him [God], and through him, and to him are all things: to whom be glory forever. Amen.

Rom. 14, 8. Whether we live, we live unto the Lord; and whether we die, we die unto the Lord: whether we live, therefore, or die, we are the Lord's.

Ps. 145, 10. All thy works shall praise thee, O Lord; and thy saints shall bless thee.

Prov. 16, 4. The Lord hath made all things for himself: yea, even the wicked for the day of evil.

1 Cor. 10, 31. Whether therefore ye eat or drink, or whatsoever ye do, do all to the glory of God.

John 17, 24. Father, I will that they also whom thou hast given me, be with me where I am; that they may behold my glory which thou hast given me.

5. *What, then, should be your chief concern in this life?*

To do the will of God, and to save my soul.

* Matt. 16, 26. What is a man profited, if he shall gain the whole world, and lose his own soul? or what shall a man give in exchange for his soul?

* Matt. 6, 33. Seek ye first the kingdom of God, and his righteousness; and all these things shall be added unto you.

Phil. 2, 12. 13. Work out your own salvation with fear and trembling. For it is God who worketh in you both to will and to do of his good pleasure.

John 5, 30. I seek not mine own will, but the will of the Father who hath sent me.—Comp. Matt. 26, 39. 42.

John 4, 34. My meat is to do the will of him that sent me, and to finish his work.

Matt. 6, 10. Thy will be done in earth as it is in heaven.

TOPICS FOR THE FIRST LESSON.—NOTES AND HINTS.

(1.) The *divine origin* and the *divine destiny of man*, who is made in the image of God and for the glory of God. "Thou, O God, hast created us for thyself, and our hearts are without rest until they rest in thee." (St. Augustine.)

(2.) The *priceless value of the immortal soul*, which exceeds the value of the whole material world. * Matt. 16, 26.

(3.) The *threefold obligation* of man to serve and glorify God, on account of his *creation* by God the Father, of his *redemption* by God the Son, and of his *regeneration* and *sanctification* by God the Holy Ghost.

(4.) The *supreme importance of religion*, as the bond which unites man to God. *Religion* means re-union and com-munion of man with God, and implies: (a) an original *union* of man with God in the state of innocence in paradise; (b) a *separation* of man from God by sin and death; (c) a *re*-union of man with God through Christ by redemption from the curse of sin and death.

II. The Way of Salvation. *Jude 21.*

1. *Is it the will of God, that you should be saved?*

It is.

2. *Why so?*

Because God is love, and will have all men to be saved.

* 1 John 4, 8. God is love.

* Ezek. 33, 11. As I live, saith the Lord God, I have no pleasure in the death of the wicked; but that the wicked turn from his way and live.—Comp. 18, 23. 32.

1 Tim. 2, 4. God will have all men to be saved, and to come unto the knowledge of the truth.

2 Pet. 3, 9. The Lord is longsuffering to us-ward, not willing that any should perish, but that all should come to repentance.

3. *How has God revealed his love to you?*

By giving his only begotten Son, our Lord and Saviour Jesus Christ.

* John 3, 16. God so loved the world that he gave his only begotten Son, that whosoever believeth in him, should not perish, but have everlasting life.

* 1 Tim. 1, 15. This is a faithful saying and worthy of all acceptation, that Christ Jesus came into the world to save sinners.

Rom. 5, 8. God commendeth his love toward us in that, while we were yet sinners, Christ died for us.

1 John 4, 9. 10; Matt. 10, 11; Luke 19, 10.

4. *Can you be saved by your own strength?*

No; but only by the grace of God in Christ.

* Acts 4, 12. Neither is there salvation in any other [but Christ]: for there is none other name under heaven given among men, whereby we must be saved.
Rom. 3, 23. 24. All have sinned, and come short of the glory of God; being justified freely by his grace through the redemption that is in Christ Jesus.
Eph. 2, 8. 9; Gal. 3, 16; Tit. 3, 5–7.

5. *What must you do to be saved?*

I must repent of my sins, and believe in Jesus Christ.

John 3, 36. He that believeth on the Son hath everlasting life.
* Mark 1, 11. Repent ye, and believe the gospel.
Mark 16, 16. He that believeth and is baptized, shall be saved; but he that believeth not, shall be damned.
Luke 9, 23. If any man will come after me, let him deny himself and take up his cross daily, and follow me.—Comp. 14, 27; Matt. 10, 38; 16, 24.
Acts 16, 30. 31. [The question of the jailer at Philippi:] "What must I do to be saved?" [and the answer of St. Paul:] "Believe on the Lord Jesus, and thou shalt be saved."

6. *Where is the way of salvation pointed out to us?*

In the Holy Scriptures.

* 2 Tim. 3, 15. From a child thou hast known the Holy Scriptures, which are able to make thee wise unto salvation through faith which is in Christ Jesus.
John 5, 39. Search the Scriptures; for in them ye think ye have eternal life: and they are they which testify of me [*i.e.* of Christ as the promised Saviour].

III. Of the Holy Scriptures.

1. *Where has God revealed himself?*

In the works of creation, in the conscience of man, and in the history of nations.

(1.) In the CREATION: * Ps. 19, 2. The heavens declare the glory of God; and the firmament showeth his handy work.— Comp. Rom. 1, 19, 20; Acts 14, 17: 17, 26–28.

(2.) In the CONSCIENCE. Rom. 2, 14. 15. When the Gentiles, who have not the [revealed Mosaic] law, do by nature the things contained in the law, these having not the law, are a [natural inward] law unto themselves: who show the work of the law written in their hearts, their conscience also bearing witness [or, the conscience witnessing with them], and their thoughts the meanwhile accusing or else excusing one another. —Comp. John 1, 9; 8, 9 (being convicted by their own conscience).

(3.) In the HISTORY of the world. Acts 14, 17. God left not himself without witness. [This was spoken to heathens.]—Comp. 17, 26–28; John 1, 5. 10. (The sacred history belongs to the revelation of God in his word, a great part of which both in the Old and New Testament consists of history.)

2. *Where has God most fully and clearly revealed himself?*

In his holy word, and in the person of our Lord and Saviour Jesus Christ.

* Ps. 119, 105. Thy word is a lamp unto my feet, and a light unto my path.—Comp. Ps. 19, 8, 9.

2 Pet. 1, 19. We have also a more sure word of prophecy; whereunto ye do well that ye take heed, as unto a light that shineth in a dark place, until the day dawn and the day star arise in your hearts.

2 Tim. 3, 15–17; Heb. 1, 1. 2; 4, 12. 13.

3. *Where is the Word of God contained?*

In the Bible, or the Holy Scriptures.

4. *What does the word Bible mean?*

The Book of books, or the best and most important of all books.

5. *Who wrote the Bible?*

Prophets and Apostles, under the inspiration of the Holy Ghost.

* 2 Pet. 1, 21. The prophecy came not in old time by the will of man; but holy men of God spake as they were moved by the Holy Ghost.

Heb. 1, 1. 2. God, who at sundry times and in divers manners spake in times past unto the fathers by the prophets, hath in these last days spoken unto us by his Son.

2 Tim. 3, 16. All Scripture is given by inspiration of God

1 Thess. 2, 13. When ye received the word of God which ye heard of us, ye received it not as the word of men, but as it is in truth, the word of God, which effectually worketh also in you that believe.

On the inspiration of the Apostles, see John 20, 22; Acts 2, 4.

6. *What are the contents of the Bible?*

The Bible contains a revelation of the triune God in the creation, the redemption, and the sanctification of the world.

7. *What benefit is the Bible to us?*

The Bible shows us the way of salvation, and is the infallible rule of the Christian faith and life.

* 2 Tim. 3, 16. 17. All Scripture is given by inspiration of God, and is profitable for doctrine, for reproof, for correction, for instruction in righteousness: that the man of God may be perfect, thoroughly furnished unto all good works.

Ps. 119, 105. Thy word is a lamp unto my feet, and a light unto my path.

Heb. 4, 12. The word of God is quick, and powerful, and sharper than any twoedged sword, piercing even to the dividing asunder of soul and spirit, and of the joints and marrow, and is a discerner of the thoughts and intents of the heart.

John 5, 39; 10, 35 (the Scripture cannot be broken); 17, 17; Rom. 15, 4; 2 Pet. 1, 19.

8. *Who enables you to understand the Bible?*

The same Holy Spirit who inspired the Bible, and is given to believers.

Ps. 119, 18. Open thou mine eyes, that I may behold wondrous things out of thy law.

* John 16, 13. When he, the Spirit of truth, is come, he will guide you into all truth.

1 Cor. 2, 14. The natural man receiveth not the things of the Spirit of God: for they are foolishness unto him: neither can he know them, because they are spiritually discerned.

1 Cor. 2, 10. But God hath revealed them unto us by his Spirit: for the Spirit searcheth all things, yea, the of God.

Luke 11, 13. If ye, being evil, know how to giv

unto your children; how much more shall your heavenly Father give the Holy Spirit to them that ask him?
Matt. 16, 17; John 14, 26; 1 John 2, 20. 27.

9. *What use should you make of the Bible?*

We should diligently and devoutly study the Bible, as the book of God, and conform to its teachings.

* Luke 11, 28. Blessed are they that hear the word of God, and keep it.

* Jam. 1, 22. Be ye doers of the word, and not hearers [or readers] only, deceiving your own selves.

John 13, 17. If ye know these things, happy are ye if ye do them. John 7, 17; 8, 31; Matt. 7, 21.

NOTES AND HINTS.

Q. 3. The Bible embraces the works of about forty authors of different classes of society, from the lowly condition of the fisherman and shepherd, to the exalted position of the lawgiver and king: it was written during the long period of sixteen hundred years (the books of Moses about fifteen hundred years *before*, the Revelation of St. John nearly one hundred years *after*, the birth of Christ), in different places, as Egypt, the Desert of Arabia, Canaan, Asia Minor, Greece, and Rome; and it contains a great variety of matter and forms of composition, as history, poetry, prophecy, proverbial philosophy, doctrine, precept, from the simplest style to the sublimest flights of diction. Yet, with all these differences, it breathes from beginning to end the same spirit, and teaches the same system of faith and practice, and the same plan and way of salvation; the apparent discrepancies being merely the successive stages of development from the germ to the flower and fruit, or from the dawn of the morning to the splendor of the noonday sun. For it exhibits the truth, not as a dead tradition or uniform repetition from age to age, but as a vital principle and living power, ever growing and expanding, and yet ever retaining its identity and essential unity. Let no one take offence at the modesty and humility of its form and language, for thus it reaches even the lowliest capacity. The word of God has indeed become flesh and blood, and assumed the form of a servant, but out of the veil of this real humanity shines forth the glory of eternal truth. The Bible, under whatever view we may regard it, is undoubtedly the most remarkable of all books, and beyond the reach of comparison. It can teach, edify, improve, terrify, comfort, and cheer as no other book. It has a creative, regenerative, sanctifying, all-penetrating power for every reader that is seriously concerned about his salvation, and pierces to the very marrow of our heart and conscience. It improves upon acquaintance, and challenges our reverence and affection in proportion as we use it. We never get tired of it, as we do of the greatest works of man. Like a torch, the more it is shaken the more it shines, and, like a healing herb, the harder it is pressed the stronger the sweet fragrance it yields. Even its difficulties and mysteries—like similar mysteries in the book of creation—have their use, and should remind us of the imperfections of our earthly knowledge, and stimulate us to deeper research. The Bible has the seal of approbation of all Christendom for these eighteen hundred years, and continually verifies itself in the experience of every Christian by the inner testimony of the Holy Spirit, who breathes through it with his supernatural power.

The Bible is a book of *life*, the book of *God*, for *all* mankind: for children and adults, for the rich and the poor, for rulers and subjects, for the learned and the illiterate, easily intelligible and yet unfathomable, old and yet ever young and fresh, as God himself, who gave it as our guide in the path of piety, virtue and happiness.

> "Within this sacred volume lies
> The mystery of mysteries.
> Oh, happy they of human race,
> To whom our God has given grace
> To hear, to read, to praise and pray,
> To lift the latch, and force the way!
> But better had they ne'er been born,
> Who read to doubt, or read to scorn."

Q. 4. The passages on the *inspiration* of the Bible refer more directly to the Old Testament, the New Testament being then not completed, but from them we may infer, *a fortiori*, the inspiration of the New, which is the fulfilment of the Old. Jesus Christ is the supreme and absolute authority for Christians, and of him the Bible bears witness from beginning to end. Heaven and earth shall pass away, but his words shall not pass away. (Matt. 24, 35.) The writings of the apostles are only the faithful reflection of his teaching under the unerring guidance of the Holy Spirit, which was given to them on the day of Pentecost. (Acts 2, 4.)

Q. 7. The Holy Spirit reveals, through faith, even to the unlearned and simple, so much of the meaning of the Scriptures as is necessary for their edification and salvation; while, without faith, it is a sealed book even to the wisest and most learned: hence the Saviour praises his heavenly Father, because he has hid these things from the wise and prudent, and revealed them unto babes. (Matt. 11, 25.)

IV. The Old and the New Testament.

1. *What are the two parts of the Bible?*

The Old and the New Testament.

2. *What does the word Testament mean?*

The covenant which God made with man.

3. *What covenants did God make with man?*

First the covenant of the law through his servant Moses, and then the covenant of the gospel through his Son Jesus Christ.

4. *What does the Old Testament contain?*

The law and the promise.

5. *What does the New Testament contain?*

The gospel, which is the fulfilment of the law, and the promise.

6. *How, then, are both related to each other?*

The Old Testament is the preparation for the New, and the New Testament is the perfection of the Old.

* Matt. 5, 17. Think not that I am come to destroy the law, or the prophets: I am not come to destroy, but to fulfil.
John 1, 17. The law was given by Moses, but grace and truth came by Jesus Christ.
Rom. 10, 4. Christ is the end of the law for righteousness to every one that believeth.

7. *In what language was the Bible originally written?*

The Old Testament was written in Hebrew, the New Testament in Greek; but both are now translated into almost every language of the world.

8. *What is the sum and substance of both Testaments?*

Jesus Christ.

* John 5, 39. They [the Scriptures] are they which testify of me [Christ].
John 1, 45. We have found him of whom Moses in the law and the prophets did write, Jesus of Nazareth.
Luke 24, 44. All things must be fulfilled, which were written in the law of Moses, and in the prophets, and in the psalms, concerning me.

NOTES AND HINTS.

Q. 2. *Testament* (from the Latin *testis*, witness) means properly the *last will* confirmed by witnesses, or a written instrument, duly certified, concerning the disposition of a person's property after death. In this sense we may say that the Gospels are the will of Christ, and the Epistles the codicils annexed; and that both constitute the supreme authority, which must decide all controversies among the descendants of the family. But in the Latin Bible, from which it passed into modern translations, *Testament* is the equivalent for the Greek *diatheke*, which means both a *will* (Heb. 9, 16. 17), and a *covenant* or agreement between two persons or parties, embracing mutual promises on mutual conditions (Gen. 15, 18; 17, 2; Luke 1, 72; Gal. 3, 15). The word was first used for the two dispensations, the Mosaic and the Christian; but since Tertullian, in the second century, it also signifies the *books* wherein they are authoritatively recorded; the sacred writings of the Jews being called the *Old Testament*, and the sacred writings of the Christians being called the *New Testament*. We should read the Testament, not as lawyers who criticize it, but as *children* who *inherit* it.

Q. 3. The *Old Covenant*, or the *Jewish* dispensation, is the covenant of *law*, made on Mount Sinai, between God and the Jewish people through Moses, with sacrifices and the blood of beasts, Ex. 24, 3–12; Deut. 5, 2–5; Gal. 3, 24. The *New Covenant*, or the *Christian* dispensation, is the covenant of the *Gospel*, promised of old, and foretold by the prophets, made between God and the whole human race through Christ ("the mediator of a better covenant"), and sealed by his blood for the remission of sins, Jer. 31, 31–34; Matt. 26, 28; Heb. 7, 22; 8, 7–13; 9, 15–17. The old dispensation was *national*, and merely *preparatory* to the Christian, and hence temporary. The new dispensation is *general* and *eternal*.

Q. 4. Hence the expression "the *law* and the *prophets*," for the whole Old Testament, Matt. 5, 17; 7, 12; 22, 40, and often.

Q. 6. The New Testament is *concealed* in the Old; the Old Testament is *revealed* in the New. They are related to each other as the germ and the fruit. Christianity is, on the one hand, the fulfilment and perfection of Judaism; but, on the other hand, it is also a new and the highest revelation, a new moral creation. At the incarnation of Christ the creative word was repeated in a higher spiritual sense: "Let there be light: and there was light."

Q. 7. The Hebrew was the vernacular language of the Jews, for whom the Old Testament revelation was originally intended. The Greek language was the ruling language in the Roman empire at the time of Christ and the Apostles. The Bible was at an early period translated into Latin, Syriac, and all other languages in which Christianity was preached. During the period of the Reformation most of the translations were made which are now used in Protestant churches. The Bible is now printed in two hundred and twenty-six different languages or dialects. More than four-fifths of these versions are the product of missionary scholarship and zeal. The British and Foreign Bible Society, founded March 7, 1804, has issued 82,407,062 copies of the Scriptures (1879). The American Bible Society, founded May 8, 1816, has issued 35,621,262 copies of the Scriptures (1879); and millions of copies have been printed and circulated by other publishers. Twice as many copies of the Bible have been circulated in the present century in heathen lands as were issued between the first printed Bible and the era of Bible Societies (1804), or about three hundred and fifty years. A number of translations of the Bible were made into English previous to the present Authorized Version, made in 1611, and a fresh revision of the New Testament, made by the Anglo-American Revision Committee, is to be issued in 1880, and a similar revision of the Old Testament is to be completed in two or three years.

V. The Old Testament.

1. How many books does the Old Testament contain?

Thirty-nine.

2. How are they divided?

Into historical, poetical, and prophetical books.

3. Name the historical books.

First, the five books of Moses, called Genesis, Exodus, Leviticus, Numbers, and Deuteronomy.

4. Name the other historical books.

Joshua, Judges, Ruth, First and Second Samuel, First and Second Kings, First and Second Chronicles, Ezra, Nehemiah, and Esther.

5. Which are the poetical books?

Job, Psalms, Proverbs, Ecclesiastes or the Preacher, and the Song of Solomon.

6. Which are the prophetical books?

The prophecies of the four greater, and the twelve minor prophets.

7. Name the greater prophets.

Isaiah, Jeremiah (with the Lamentations), Ezekiel, and Daniel.

8. Name the minor prophets.

Hosea, Joel, Amos, Obadiah, Jonah, Micah, Nahum, Habakkuk, Zephaniah, Haggai, Zechariah, and Malachi.

9. What are all these books called?

The canonical books of the Old Testament.

10. *Why so?*

Because they are divinely inspired, and, together with the New Testament, constitute the rule of faith.

Notes and Hints.

Q. 2. The Old Testament is popularly divided into *Moses* and the *Prophets*. More accurately, it is divided into three classes of books:— (1.) The *historical* books relate the history of the divine revelation, and the fortunes of the people of God from the creation down to the return from the Babylonish captivity. (2.) The *poetical* books, sometimes also called the *didactic* books, exhibit the religion of the Old Testament in sacred poems, prayers, and proverbs. (3.) The *prophetical* books contain exhortations, warnings, and predictions of future events, especially of the coming of the Messiah for the salvation of Israel and the whole human race.

Q. 9 and 10. The *canonical* books (from the Greek word *canon*, i.e. rule or measure) are so called to distinguish them from the *Apocrypha*, or obscure books, which are added to all the Roman Catholic and also to many Protestant editions of the Bible. These apocryphal books are useful and edifying, and form an important historical link between the Old and the New Testament, but are not inspired, and hence no part of the rule of the Christian faith, for the following reason: (1.) The apocryphal books were written by *unknown* authors *after the extinction of prophecy* (Malachi) and *after the collection of the Jewish canon* by Ezra and Nehemiah, not in the Hebrew language, as the canonical books, but originally in Greek. (2.) They were not regarded by the Jews (according to Josephus), nor by the primitive Christians before Augustine, as belonging to the sacred canon or the body of inspired and authoritative books. Even Jerome (who was a better Biblical scholar than Augustine) insists upon the distinction. (3.) They are never quoted by Christ and the Apostles in the New Testament. (4.) They contain, with many remarkable providences and elevated doctrinal and moral sentences, also a number of historical and doctrinal errors. For these reasons, they should either be distinguished from the canonical books by smaller type, or be excluded from the editions of the Bible. The latter is the policy of the British and American Bible Societies.

The Jewish Apocrypha are twelve or more in number, viz., Wisdom of Solomon, Ecclesiasticus (or the Wisdom of Jesus the Son of Sirach), Tobit, Judith, the Rest of Esther, Baruch, the Song of the Three Children, the Story of Susanna, Bel and the Dragon (sometimes divided into two books), the Prayer of Manasses, two books of the Maccabees; to which some editions of the Bible add a third book of the Maccabees, and several books of Esdras.

VI. The New Testament.

1. *How many books does the New Testament contain?*

Twenty-seven.

2. *How is the New Testament divided?*

Into historical, doctrinal, and prophetical books.

3. *Which are the historical books of the New Testament?*

The four Gospels and the Acts.

4. *Who wrote the Gospels?*

The Evangelists Matthew, Mark, Luke, and John.

5. *What does the word Gospel mean?*

The glad tidings of salvation in Christ.

* Rom. 1, 16. I am not ashamed of the gospel of Christ: for it is the power of God unto salvation to every one that believeth.

Luke 2, 10. 11. And the angel said unto them [the shepherds of Bethlehem]: Fear not; for, behold, I bring you good tidings of great joy, which shall be to all people. For unto you is born this day, in the city of David, a Saviour, which is Christ the Lord.

Mark 16, 15. Go ye into all the world, and preach the gospel to every creature.

6. *What do the Gospels treat of?*

The life and doctrine, the death and resurrection, of Jesus Christ.

7. *Who is the author of the Acts of the Apostles?*

Luke, the Evangelist.

8. *What do the Acts contain?*

The history of the founding and spread of Christianity under the Apostles, especially St. Peter and St. Paul.

9. *Which are the doctrinal or didactic books?*

Fourteen epistles of Paul, and seven catholic or general epistles.

10. *Name the Epistles of St. Paul.*

The Epistle to the Romans, First and Second Corinthians, Galatians, Ephesians, Philippians, Colossians, First and Second Thessalonians, First and Second Timothy, Titus, Philemon, and Hebrews.

11. *Name the catholic or general Epistles.*

Two Epistles of Peter, three of John, one of James, and one of Jude.

12. *What do the doctrinal books treat of?*

The Christian faith and life.

13. *Which is the prophetical book of the New Testament?*

The Revelation of St. John.

14. *What are the contents of the book of Revelation?*

A prophetical description of the conflicts and triumphs of the Christian Church till the glorious coming of Christ.

NOTES AND HINTS.

Q. 5. The English word *gospel*, from the old Saxon *God's spell* (speech), or *good spell*, means *good news* or *glad tidings*, and is the precise equivalent for the Greek word *evangelion*, from which we derive the verb *to evangelize*.

Q. 10. The Epistle to the Hebrews is anonymous, and the opinions of divines as to its author are divided. But, if not directly the work of St. Paul, it proceeded from one of his disciples, and breathes his spirit throughout.

Q. 14. The Revelation of Christ through St. John, or the Apocalypse, forms the fit conclusion to the canon. The whole New Testament is a beautiful organism, in which the Gospels may be compared to the root, the Epistles to the branches, the Revelation to the ripe fruit. Or, to use another figure, the first form the foundation, the second the edifice itself, and the last the dome. The three classes bear to each other the same relation as conversion, sanctification, and glorification, or as the cardinal Christian virtues, faith, love, and hope. The substance, the all-absorbing theme, the beginning, middle, and end, of the whole Testament, is JESUS CHRIST.

PART FIRST.

The Lord's Prayer.

VII. Of Prayer.

1. *What is prayer?*

The raising of the heart to God, and communing with him.

* Ps. 19, 14. Let the words of my mouth, and the meditation of my heart, be acceptable in thy sight, O Lord, my strength and my redeemer.
Ps. 62, 8. Pour out your heart before him; God is a refuge for us.

2. *Why should we pray?*

Because God commands us to pray, and because we are poor, needy creatures, who receive all temporal and spiritual gifts from the goodness of God.

* James 1, 17. Every good gift and every perfect gift is from above, and cometh down from the Father of lights.
1 Cor. 4, 7. What hast thou that thou didst not receive?
1 Cor. 15, 10. By the grace of God I am what I am.
John 3, 27. A man can receive nothing except it be given him from heaven.
Ps. 50, 15. Call upon me in the day of trouble: I will deliver thee, and thou shalt glorify me.—Matt. 7, 7.

3. *Is prayer simply a duty?*

It is not only a sacred duty, but also a precious privilege of the children of God.

4. *What are the different kinds of prayer?*

Adoration, thanksgiving, intercession, petition, and praise.

* 1 Tim. 2, 1. I exhort therefore, that, first of all, supplications, prayers, intercessions, and giving of thanks be made for all men.
Phil. 4, 6.

5. *To whom should we pray?*

Only to God, who is both able and willing to give us all we need.

* Matt. 4, 10. Thou shalt worship the Lord thy God, and him only shalt thou serve.—Comp. Rev. 19, 10; 22, 8. 9.
Eph. 3, 20. 21. Unto him that is able to do exceeding abundantly above all that we ask or think, according to the power that worketh in us, unto him be glory in the church by Christ Jesus throughout all ages, world without end.—Comp. Ps. 65, 3; James 1, 17.

6. *How should we pray?*

In the name of Christ, humbly and devoutly, with childlike faith in God's mercy, and resignation to his holy will.

* John 16, 23. Verily, verily, I say unto you, Whatsoever ye shall ask the Father in my name, he will give it you.—Comp. 14, 13.
John 4, 24. God is a Spirit; and they that worship him, must worship him in spirit and in truth.
Matt. 21, 22. All things, whatsoever ye shall ask in prayer, believing, ye shall receive.—Comp. Mark 11, 24; James 1, 6. 7; 5, 16.
Heb. 4, 16. Let us come boldly unto the throne of grace.
Heb. 10, 22. Let us draw near with a true heart in full assurance of faith.
Matt. 26, 39. Not as I will, but as thou wilt.

7. *For what should we pray?*

For all spiritual and temporal blessings, but not for any thing which is contrary to the will of God.

See the Lord's Prayer.

OF PRAYER. 25

8. *For whom should we pray?*

For ourselves, for our parents, kindred and friends, and for all men, even our enemies.

* 1 Tim. 2, 1. 2. I exhort therefore, that, first of all, supplications, prayers, intercessions, and giving of thanks be made for all men; for kings, and for all that are in authority; that we may lead a quiet and peaceable life in all godliness and honesty.

Ps. 122, 6. Pray for the peace of Jerusalem: they shall prosper that love thee.

James 5, 16. Pray one for another.

* Matt. 5, 44. 45. Love your enemies, bless them that curse you, do good to them that hate you, and pray for them which despitefully use you, and persecute you; that ye may be the children of your Father which is in heaven: for he maketh his sun to rise on the evil and on the good, and sendeth rain on the just and on the unjust.

9. *Where can and should we pray?*

Everywhere, but especially in the church, in the family, and in the closet.

(1.) PUBLIC prayer. Ps. 122, 1. 2. Let us go into the house of the Lord. Our feet shall stand within thy gates, O Jerusalem. Acts 3, 1. Peter and John went up together into the temple at the hour of prayer. Heb. 10, 25. Not forsaking the assembling of ourselves together, as the manner of some is; but exhorting one another.

(2.) SOCIAL and FAMILY prayer. Matt. 18, 20. Where two or three are gathered together in my name, there am I in the midst of them.—Comp. Acts 1, 14; 2, 46 (from house to house); 12, 12 (the house of Mary the mother of John, ... where many were gathered together praying).

(3.) PRIVATE prayer. Matt. 6, 6. When thou prayest, enter into thy closet, and when thou hast shut thy door, pray to thy Father which is in secret; and thy Father which seeth in secret, shall reward thee openly.—Comp. Mark 1, 35; Ps. 55, 17; Dan. 6, 10.

10. *How often should we pray?*

At all times, but especially every morning and evening, and at every meal.

* 1 Thess. 5, 17. Pray without ceasing.—Comp. Luke 18, 1; Eph. 6, 18; Rom. 12, 12.

* Ps. 55, 17. Evening, and morning, and at noon will I pray, and cry aloud: and he shall hear my voice.

Ps. 92, 1. 2. It is a good thing to give thanks unto the Lord, and to sing praises unto thy name, O most High: to show forth thy loving-kindness in the morning, and thy faithfulness every night.

Dan. 6, 10. Daniel . . . kneeled upon his knees three times a day, and prayed, and gave thanks before his God, as he did aforetime.—Comp. Acts 2, 1. 2. 15; 3, 1; 10, 9.

1 Tim. 4, 4. Every creature of God is good, and nothing to be refused, if it be received with thanksgiving: for it is sanctified by the word of God and prayer.

Rom. 14, 6. He that eateth, eateth to the Lord, for he giveth God thanks.—Comp. 1 Cor. 10, 30. 31; Deut. 8, 10; and the example of Christ, John 6, 11; Matt. 26, 26.

11. *Does God hear our prayers?*

God hears all our prayers, for he is omnipresent and omniscient.

Ps. 145, 18. The Lord is nigh unto all them that call upon him, to all that call upon him in truth. Comp. Ps. 139, 7-12; Eph. 3, 20.

12. *Does God answer our prayers?*

God answers our prayers for Christ's sake, because he is our merciful Father.

* Matt. 7, 7. Ask, and it shall be given you; seek, and ye shall find; knock, and it shall be opened unto you.

* John 14, 14. If ye shall ask any thing in my name, I will do it.

James 5, 16. The effectual fervent prayer of the righteous man availeth much.

Ps. 10, 17; 34, 15; 50, 15; 91, 14. 15; 145, 9. 18; Prov. 15, 29; Matt. 21, 22; John 16, 23; Luke 11, 11-13; Eph. 3, 20.

13. *But when does God refuse our prayers?*

When we ask amiss, or for things injurious to us.

* James 4, 3. Ye ask, and receive not, because ye ask amiss, that ye may consume it upon your lusts.

James 1, 6. 7. Let him ask in faith, nothing wavering. For he that wavereth is like a wave of the sea driven with the wind

OF PRAYER.

and tossed. For let not that man think that he shall receive any thing of the Lord.

Ps. 66, 18. If I regard iniquity in my heart, the Lord will not hear me.

* Prov. 15, 29. The Lord is far from the wicked; but he beareth the prayer of the righteous.

Job 27, 9; Isa. 1, 15; Jer. 11, 11; Micah 3, 4; Prov. 1, 28; John 9, 31.

NOTES AND HINTS.

We commence with an exposition of prayer, and the Lord's Prayer, contrary to catechetical usage, but agreeably to the natural order of religious education; children being first taught the Lord's Prayer, then the Creed, and last the Ten Commandments.

Q. 2. Prayer may be considered (1) as an essential *want* of every religious man, even the heathen and Mohammedan; (2) as a sacred *duty* enjoined in the word of God; (3) as a precious *privilege* and source of unspeakable benefit.

Q. 5. As a general rule, prayer is addressed *to God the Father* (as in the Lord's Prayer), *in the name of Christ, through the Holy Spirit*, who enables us to pray, and intercedes for us with unutterable groanings (Rom. 8, 26). But Christ and the Holy Spirit being strictly divine in essence and character, they may also be *directly* addressed in prayer, as was done by the dying Stephen, Acts 7, 59. 61; comp. 1 Cor. 1, 2 (all that call upon the name of Jesus Christ our Lord); Acts 9, 14. 21; 22, 16; Phil. 2, 9; 2 Tim. 2, 22; Heb. 1, 6; Rev. 5, 11–13.

As to the *invocation* of *angels* and *departed saints*, it is nowhere authorized in the Scriptures, either by precept or example, and expressly censured in Rev. 19, 10 and 22, 8. 9. Christ is our only and all-sufficient mediator and advocate with the Father, and his merits and intercession far exceed in value and effect the combined merits and intercessions of all saints.—Comp. John 14, 6; 1 John 2, 1. 2; 1 Tim. 2, 5; Heb. 7, 25; Eph. 2, 18. It is the glorious privilege of the evangelical Christian to commune directly and personally with Christ without the intervening influence of others. To saints belong honor and grateful remembrance, but worship and adoration are due to God alone.

Q. 6. The *length* of a prayer is of small account. God looks to the heart. Better few words and much devotion, than many words and little devotion.—Comp. Matt. 6, 7. The prayer of the publican in the temple (Luke 18, 13), and the Lord's Prayer, are short. Yet the Lord himself, in the days of his flesh, spent whole nights in prayer, Luke 6, 12; comp. 5, 16; Mark 1, 35.

The *posture* in prayer is likewise unessential, whether it be with folded hands, or stretched-out arms, or standing, or on bended knees. But it should always be *reverential;* that is, expressive of a devotional frame of mind, and a sense of the presence of God.

Q. 12. Striking *examples* of *answers* to prayer are furnished by the history of *Abraham*, Gen. 20, 17; *Jacob*, 32, 24–31 (his wrestling in prayer); *Moses*, Num. 11, 2; Deut. 9, 19; *Joshua*, Josh. 10, 12; *Samuel*, 1 Sam. 12, 18; *Elijah*, 1 Kings 17, 1; 18, 42. 45; *Elisha*, 2 Kings 4, 33. 34; *Hezekiah*, 2 Kings 19, 15–20; 20, 2–6; the *woman of Canaan*, Matt. 15, 21–28; the *penitent thief*, Luke 23, 42. 43; the *Apostles*, Acts 4, 31; *Peter* in prison, 12, 8. 12; *Paul* and *Silas* at Philippi, 16, 25. 26, etc.

Q. 13. Sometimes the Lord refuses also the petitions of *believers* when offered in the *name* of Christ; but he does so only apparently, and with the view to answer them at a better *time* or in a better *manner* than they wished in their short-sightedness. *Examples:* the *sisters of Lazarus*, John 11, 1–45; *Jairus*, Luke 8, 49–56; *St. Paul*, 2 Cor. 12, 8. 9. *Monica*, the mother of Augustine, prayed for thirty years for the conversion of her great son, and was finally heard beyond her boldest expectations. When he took passage to Italy, she asked the Lord to frustrate his designs, fearing that he might expose himself to still greater danger; but the Lord prospered his voyage and made it the occasion for his conversion, thus hearing the substance or intent of her prayer, while denying its form.

VIII. The Lord's Prayer.

1. *Which is the model prayer?*

The Lord's Prayer, which Jesus himself taught his disciples.

Matt. 6, 9–13; Luke 11, 1–4.

2. *Repeat the Lord's Prayer.*

Our Father who art in heaven:

Hallowed be thy name. Thy kingdom come. Thy will be done in earth as *it is* in heaven. Give us this day our daily bread. And forgive us our debts, as we forgive our debtors. And lead us not into temptation, but deliver us from evil.

For thine is the kingdom, and the power, and the glory, forever. Amen.

3. *How many parts has the Lord's Prayer?*

Three parts: an address, six petitions, and a doxology.

4. *How do you divide the petitions?*

Into two classes, each consisting of three petitions.

5. *What do the first three petitions refer to?*

To the riches and glory of God, which

we call down in prayer from heaven upon earth.

Hence: *Thy* name, *thy* kingdom, *thy* will.

6. *What do the last three petitions refer to?*

To the poverty and need of man, from which we ascend to God in prayer.

Hence: *Our* daily bread, *our* debts, *our* temptations and deliverance.

Note.

The *Lord's Prayer* is the Prayer of prayers, as the Bible is the Book of books, and the Apostles' Creed, the Creed of creeds. It is the best and most beautiful, the simplest and yet the deepest, the shortest and yet the most comprehensive, of all forms of devotion. Only from the lips of the Son of God could such a perfect pattern proceed. An ancient father calls it a summary of Christianity, or the gospel in a nutshell. It embraces all kinds of prayer,—petition, intercession, and thanksgiving; all essential objects of prayer, spiritual and temporal, divine and human, in the most suitable and beautiful order, commencing with the glory of God, gradually descending to man's needs, then rising to the final deliverance from all evil, and ending in thanksgiving and praise, as all prayer must end at last, in heaven, where all our wants shall be supplied. It accompanies the Christian from the cradle to the grave. It can never be superseded. If we have exhausted the whole extent of our religious wants, and the whole vocabulary of devotion, we gladly return to this model prayer, as infinitely superior to all our own effusions. It may, indeed, be abused, like every gift of God, and become a dead form. Luther called it in this respect "the greatest martyr on earth." This is equally true of the whole Bible, the most abused of all books. But this is no argument against its proper and frequent use. It is not intended, of course, to supersede other forms, or extemporaneous prayers; but it should serve as a general pattern and directory to all our devotions, and breathe into them the proper spirit. It should be the key-note of all Christian prayers. It is "the concert-pitch of the universal heavenly choir of the whole family on earth and in heaven."

IX. The Address.

1. *What is the address of the Lord's Prayer?*

Our Father who art in heaven.

2. *Why do you address God as Father?*

Because he is in Christ our reconciled Father, and because we should approach him with childlike reverence and trust.

Ps. 103, 13. Like as a father pitieth his children, so the Lord pitieth them that fear him.

* Gal. 3, 26. Ye are all the children of God by faith in Christ Jesus.

Rom. 8, 14. 15. As many as are led by the Spirit of God, they are the sons of God. For ye have not received the spirit of bondage again to fear; but ye have received the Spirit of adoption, whereby we cry, Abba, Father.—Comp. Gal. 4, 6.

John 1, 12. 13. As many as received him, to them gave he power to become the sons of God, even to them that believe on his name: which were born, not of blood, nor of the will of the flesh, nor of the will of man, but of God.

Matt. 7, 11. If ye then, being evil, know how to give good gifts unto your children, how much more shall your Father which is in heaven give good things to them that ask him?

3. *Why do you say, " Our Father," and not, " My Father"?*

Because we should pray not only for ourselves, but also for our brethren, and for all the children of God.

* James 5, 16. Pray one for another,

1 Thess. 5, 25. Brethren, pray for us.

Eph. 3, 15. The Father of our Lord Jesus Christ, of whom the whole family in heaven and earth is named.

1 Tim. 2, 1–4; Rom. 1, 9; Col. 4, 3; 2 Thess. 3, 1; Matt. 5, 44.

4. *Why do you add, "who art in heaven"?*

Because God is far above any earthly father, and because in prayer we should raise the heart to heaven, where God dwells in eternal glory, and where is our true home.

* Phil. 3, 20. Our conversation is in heaven.

* Col. 3, 2. Set your affection on things above, not on things on the earth.

Eph. 2, 6. God hath raised us up together and made us sit together in heavenly places in Christ Jesus.

Eph. 2, 19. Ye are no more strangers and foreigners, but fellow-citizens with the saints, and of the household of God.

5. *Is not God also on earth?*

God is everywhere: the heaven is his throne, and the earth is his footstool.

Isa. 66, 1; Matt. 5, 34. 35; 1 Kings 8, 27.

NOTE.

The address in the Lord's Prayer introduces us at once into the very heart of the Christian religion. It contains three important ideas. The word *Father*—the most endearing and attractive name under which God Almighty may be known, but which can only be properly appreciated and enjoyed in the gospel dispensation—teaches us the *paternal* relation which he sustains to us in Christ, and the *filial* relation which we sustain to him by faith in Christ, his *only-begotten* and *eternal* Son; the word *our* refers to the *brotherly* relation of Christians to each other, or the communion of saints; and the words *who art in heaven* remind us of our *celestial destination*. It is *faith* which prays, *Father*; *love* which prays, *our*; and *hope* which adds, *who art in heaven*. The three cardinal Christian graces unite harmoniously in every true prayer. The full meaning of this address could not be understood by the disciples before the outpouring of the Holy Spirit.

X. The First Three Petitions.

1. *What is the first petition of the Lord's Prayer?*

Hallowed be Thy name.

2. *What does this mean?*

Grant that all may rightly know and worship Thee, the only true and living God, and glorify Thee in thought, word, and deed.

* Isa. 6, 3. Holy, holy, holy, is the Lord of hosts: the whole earth is full of his glory. [The Trisagion, or the song of the seraphim.]

John 17, 3. This is life eternal, that they might know thee the only true God, and Jesus Christ whom thou hast sent.

Ps. 83, 18. That men may know that thou, whose name alone is Jehovah, art the most high over all the earth.

Matt. 4, 10. Thou shalt worship the Lord thy God, and him only shalt thou serve.

Ps. 92, 1. It is a good thing to give thanks unto the Lord, and to sing praises unto thy name, O Most High.—Comp. Ps. 51, 15; 87, 2. 3; 143, 6–8.

* Matt. 5, 16. Let your light so shine before men, that they may see your good works, and glorify your Father which is in heaven.

1 Cor. 10, 31. Whether therefore ye eat, or drink, or whatsoever ye do, do all to the glory of God.

John 15, 8; 1 Pet. 2, 12.

3. *How is God's name dishonored?*

By cursing and swearing; by ingratitude to God, and contempt of his word and authority; by false doctrine and wicked practice.

Rom. 2, 24. The name of God is blasphemed among the Gentiles through you.
Exod. 20, 7; Ezek. 5, 6; 36, 20. 23.

4. *What is the second petition?*

Thy kingdom come.

5. *What does this mean?*

Reign in us more and more by Thy Holy Spirit, and spread the gospel over the whole world, until all nations shall be converted unto Thee and serve Thee in holiness and righteousness.

* Matt. 6, 33. Seek ye first the kingdom of God and his righteousness; and all these things shall be added unto you.
Matt. 13, 31. 32. The kingdom of heaven is like to a grain of mustard seed, which a man took and sowed in his field: which indeed is the least of all seeds: but when it is grown it is the greatest among herbs, and becometh a tree, so that the birds of the air come and lodge in the branches thereof.
Luke 17, 21. The kingdom of God is within you.
John 18, 36. My kingdom is not of this world.
Rom. 14, 17. The kingdom of God is not meat and drink; but righteousness, and peace, and joy in the Holy Ghost.
1 Cor. 15, 28. When all things shall be subdued unto him, then shall the Son also himself be subject unto him that put all things under him, that God may be all in all.
Rev. 11, 15. The kingdoms of this world are become the kingdoms of our Lord, and of his Christ; and he shall reign for ever and ever.
Dan. 2, 44; 7, 14. 18. 27; Luke 1, 33.

6. *Why should we pray for the coming of the kingdom of God, since it has already come in Christ?*

Because we ourselves are not yet perfect, and because a great part of mankind are either ignorant of Christ, or Christians only in name

Matt. 9, 37. 38. The harvest truly is plenteous, but the laborers are few: pray ye therefore the Lord of the harvest, that he will send forth laborers into his harvest.

2 Thess. 3, 1; Rom. 10, 1; 11, 25.

7. *Who are not Christians?*

The heathen, Jews, Mohammedans, and infidels.

8. *Who are Christians only in name?*

Those who profess Christ with their lips, but deny him in their lives.

* Matt. 7, 21. Not every one that saith unto me, Lord, Lord, shall enter into the kingdom of heaven; but he that doeth the will of my Father which is in heaven.

2 Tim. 3, 5. Having the form of godliness, but denying the power thereof.

Tit. 1, 16. They profess that they know God; but in works they deny him, being abominable and disobedient, and unto every good work reprobate.

9. *What is the third petition?*

Thy will be done on earth as it is in heaven.

10. *What does this mean?*

Grant that we may renounce our own evil will, and cheerfully obey Thine only good and perfect will, even as the angels and saints do in heaven.

* Luke 22, 42. Not my will, but thine be done.

Heb. 13, 20. 21. Now the God of peace, that brought again from the dead our Lord Jesus, that great Shepherd of the sheep, through the blood of the everlasting covenant, make you perfect in every good work to do his will, working in you that which is well pleasing in his sight, through Jesus Christ.

* 1 John 2, 17. The world passeth away, and the lust thereof: but he that doeth the will of God, abideth forever.

Ps. 103, 20. Bless the Lord, ye his angels, that excel in strength, that do his commandments, hearkening unto the voice of his word.

THE FIRST THREE PETITIONS.

11. *What is the will of God concerning us?*

That we should be holy, even as he is holy, and that by faith in Christ we should obtain eternal life.

* Matt. 5, 48. Be ye perfect, even as your Father which is in heaven is perfect.

* Levit. 11, 44. Ye shall be holy; for I am holy.

1 Thess. 4, 3. This is the will of God, even your sanctification.

John 6, 40. This is the will of him that sent me, that every one which seeth the Son and believeth on him, may have everlasting life.

NOTES AND HINTS.

Q. 2. The *name* of God is God himself and his attributes, as far as he has named or revealed himself to man in the works of creation, redemption, and sanctification, and includes all that we know of him. Comp. John 17, 4. 6. Hence the sanctification of God's name implies also the sanctification of his holy word, his holy day, and all his ordinances.

Q. 5. The kingdom of God is: (1) the kingdom of *nature* or of *power*, which embraces all his creatures (Ps. 103, 19: "his kingdom ruleth over all"); (2) the kingdom of *grace*, or the church *militant* on earth, where God rules in Christ through the means of grace over his people, and prepares them for heaven (Col. 1, 12–14; Rom. 14, 17; Matt. 13, 31. 32); (3) the kingdom of *glory*, or the church *triumphant* in heaven, which shall appear in its full splendor at the second coming of Christ, and last forever (Matt. 25, 34: "inherit the kingdom prepared for you from the foundation of the world;" 1 Cor. 15, 25–28; Rev. 11, 15). It is the spiritual kingdom of grace and of glory to which the petition refers. The kingdom of *Satan* and of *darkness* stands opposed to the kingdom of God, but must ultimately subserve the will and glory of God.

Q. 7. *Heathenism (paganism, idolatry)*, with its various forms and ramifications, is essentially false religion, grown wild as it were on the soil of fallen human nature, yet groping in the dark after the "unknown God." It may be compared to the prodigal son, who wastes his inheritance by riotous living, but retains, even in his deepest degradation, some recollection of his father's house. In *Judaism* we must carefully distinguish between that which preceded, and that which followed the introduction of Christianity. Ancient Judaism, as laid down in the Scriptures of the Old Testament, was a preparation for the true religion by law and prophecy; post-Christian Judaism is but a ruin of the old, though a most remarkable one,—a body from which the true life has departed, and which looks in vain for the coming of the Messiah. *Mohammedanism (Islam)* is an eclectic religion, a mixture of Jewish, heathen, and a few apocryphal Christian elements,—a sort of bastard Judaism on a sensual heathen foundation; as Ishmael, the father of the Arabs, was a son of Abraham, but of the slave Hagar, and a true son of the wilderness.

Heathenism still embraces the greatest part of the human race, especially in Asia and Africa, the empire of China alone containing over three hundred millions of souls. Christianity is the religion of nearly all Europe and America, and controls at the same time the entire progress of history and civilization. Mohammedanism has its main seat in Turkey, but is gradually sinking into decay. Judaism is spread all over the earth.

The religious statistics of the globe, according to the most recent estimates (1880), are as follows:

Jews	7,000,000
Mohammedans	230,000,000
Pagans	794,000,000
Roman Catholics	216,000,000
Eastern Churches	84,000,000
Protestants	130,000,000
Total	1,461,000,000

XI. The Last Three Petitions.

1. *What is the fourth petition?*

Give us this day our daily bread.

2. *What does this mean?*

Grant us all things necessary for the body; make us content with little, and grateful for all Thy gifts.

* Ps. 145, 15. 16. The eyes of all wait upon thee; and thou givest them their meat in due season. Thou openest thine hand and satisfiest the desire of every living thing.—Comp. Ps. 37, 25; James 1, 17.

Prov. 30, 8. Give me neither poverty nor riches; feed me with food convenient for me.

Matt. 6, 34. Take no [anxious] thought for the morrow: for the morrow shall take thought for the things of itself. Sufficient unto the day is the evil thereof.

1 Tim. 6, 6–8. Godliness with contentment is great gain. For we brought nothing into this world, and it is certain we can carry nothing out. And having food and raiment, let us be therewith content.

Deut. 8, 10. When thou hast eaten and art full, then thou shalt bless the Lord for the good land he hath given thee.—Comp. the example of Christ, John 6, 11; Matt. 26, 26.

1 Tim. 4, 4. 5. Every creature of God is good and nothing to be refused, if it be received with thanksgiving; for it is sanctified by the word of God and prayer.

3. *What is the fifth petition?*

Forgive us our debts, as we forgive our debtors.

4. *What does this mean?*

Cleanse us from all our sins through the blood of Jesus Christ our Saviour.

* Luke 18, 13. God, be merciful to me a sinner.

Ps. 51, 1. 2. Have mercy upon me, O God, according to thy loving kindness: according unto the multitude of thy tender mercies blot out my transgressions. Wash me thoroughly from mine iniquity, and cleanse me from my sin.

John 1, 29. Behold the Lamb of God, which taketh away the sin of the world.

* 1 John 1, 7. The blood of Christ his Son cleanseth us from all sin.

Eph. 1, 7. In whom we have redemption through his blood, the forgiveness of sins, according to the riches of his grace.

5. *Why do you add: as we forgive our debtors?*

Because we cannot expect forgiveness of our sins from God unless we ourselves are also ready from the heart to forgive our neighbor, and to do good even to our enemies.

* Matt. 6, 14. 15. If ye forgive men their trespasses, your heavenly Father will also forgive you: but if ye forgive not men their trespasses, neither will your Father forgive your trespasses.

Matt. 18, 21. 22. Then came Peter to him, and said, Lord, how oft shall my brother sin against me, and I forgive him? till seven times? Jesus said unto him, I say not unto thee, Until seven times: but, Until seventy times seven.—Comp. Luke 17, 3. 4.

* Rom. 12, 20. 21. If thine enemy hunger, feed him; if he thirst, give him drink: for in so doing thou shalt heap coals of fire on his head. Be not overcome of evil, but overcome evil with good.

Luke 17, 3. 4; Matt. 5, 44; 18, 32. 33; James 2. 13.

Examples of conciliatory and forgiving disposition: Christ on the cross praying for his murderers, Luke 23. 34, and Stephen, doing likewise, Acts 7, 59. Example of unforgiving and implacable disposition: the wicked servant in the parable, Matt. 18, 23–35.

6. *What is the sixth petition?*

Lead us not into temptation, but deliver us from evil.

THE LAST THREE PETITIONS.

7. *What does this mean?*

Guard and strengthen us against the temptations of the flesh, the world, and the devil, and save us at last in heaven, where we shall be free from all sin and evil, and enjoy thee forever.

* Matt. 26, 41. Watch and pray, that ye enter not into temptation: the spirit indeed is willing, but the flesh is weak.

Gal. 5, 17. The flesh lusteth against the Spirit, and the Spirit against the flesh.

1 John 2, 15. Love not the world, neither the things that are in the world.—[Comp. v. 16: the lust of the flesh, the lust of the eyes, and the pride of life.]

1 John 5, 4. Whatsoever is born of God overcometh the world: and this is the victory that overcometh the world, even our faith.

1 Pet. 5, 8. Be sober, be vigilant; because your adversary the devil, as a roaring lion, walketh about, seeking whom he may devour.—Comp. Eph. 6, 11–13; James 4, 7; Gen. 3, 1–5; Matt. 4, 1–9.

* 2 Tim. 4, 7. 8. I have fought a good fight, I have finished my course, I have kept the faith: henceforth there is laid up for me a crown of righteousness, which the Lord, the righteous judge, shall give me at that day.

Ps. 31, 5. Into thine hand I commit my spirit: thou hast redeemed me, O Lord God of truth.

2 Tim. 4, 18. The Lord shall deliver me from every evil work, and will preserve me unto his heavenly kingdom: to whom be glory for ever and ever. Amen.

8. *What is the doxology?*

Thine is the kingdom, and the power, and the glory, forever.

9. *What does this mean?*

That God is both able and willing to give us all good things, and that we should give him all the glory and praise for ever and ever.

1 Chron. 29, 11. 12. Thine, O Lord, is the greatness, and the power, and the glory, and the victory, and the majesty: for all that is in the heaven and in the earth is thine; thine is the

kingdom, O Lord, and thou art exalted as head above all. Both riches and honor come of thee, and thou reignest over all; and in thy hand is power and might; and in thine hand it is to make great, and to give strength unto all.

* Eph. 3, 20. 21. Unto him that is able to do exceeding abundantly above all that we ask or think, according to the power that worketh in us, unto him be glory in the church by Christ Jesus throughout all ages, world without end.

* Ps. 115, 1. Not unto us, O Lord, not unto us, but unto thy name give glory, for thy mercy and for thy truth's sake.

10. *What do you express by the concluding word, Amen?*

My fervent desire and strong faith in God, who is faithful and true, that he will surely answer my prayer.

* 2 Cor. 1, 20. All the promises of God in him are yea, and in him Amen, unto the glory of God by us.

Isa. 65, 24. And it shall come to pass, that before they call, I will answer; and while they are yet speaking, I will hear.

2 Tim. 2, 13. If we believe not, yet he abideth faithful; he cannot deny himself.

NOTES AND HINTS.

Q. 2. This is the only petition refering to our bodily and temporal wants, which should therefore be entirely subordinated in prayer to our spiritual wants. *Daily bread* includes all that belongs to the necessities of our temporal life, as food, raiment, and clothing, but excludes all which lies beyond. It occupies thus the happy medium between poverty and riches. It is called *bread*, because bread is the most essential and valuable article of food; *daily*, because we need it from day to day; *this day* is added, because we should not anxiously care for the morrow, but trust to God for the future.

Q. 4. Sins are called *debts*, because we are *obliged* to keep God's commandments, and because sins must be either *paid*, or *atoned*, or *forgiven*. Since we can neither pay nor atone for our sins, but, on the contrary, daily increase our guilt, we ask that they may be forgiven us for Christ's sake, who by his bloody sacrifice on the cross has fully paid and atoned for the sin of the whole world, and thus satisfied the justice of God.

Q. 6. The *Reformed* catechisms and commentators (following Chrysostom) number but six petitions, because the words: *Deliver us from evil* form grammatically one sentence with the preceding petition and complete the idea, and because of the numerical correspondence of the two classes of petitions. But the *Lutherans* (following Augustin) generally regard the words referred to as a separate petition, and hence number seven petitions, in view of the comprehensive meaning of the word *evil* (including all the *consequences* of sin), and also in view of the sacredness of the number seven. The difference, however, has no religious importance. The word *evil* is by some understood of the *evil one*, the devil: by others, of *sin* with all its *effects*; by others, of *misery*. The second interpretation is the correct one.

THE LAST THREE PETITIONS. 39

Q. 10. The Hebrew word *Amen* (i.e. *truly, verily*) was the conclusion of prayer according to ancient Jewish custom. It is a word of devout *desire: May* it be; a word of certain *faith*: It *must* be; and a word of confident *hope*: It *shall* be.

If we now look back once more to the whole prayer, we must admire its order, symmetry, and completeness. Its symmetrical arrangement seems to be based on the sacred number three, in allusion to the mystery of the Holy Trinity. The division into *address—petitions*—and *thanksgiving*, is threefold; the address, *Our—Father—in heaven*, is threefold; the doxology, *kingdom—power—glory*, is threefold; and so are both classes of petitions. Between the first three and the last three petitions, moreover, there is a beautiful correspondence. The first and the fourth petitions—the name of God, and the daily bread—naturally refer mainly to God as the Creator and Preserver (the Father); the second and the fifth petitions—the kingdom of God, and the forgiveness of sins—to God the Saviour and Redeemer (the Son); the third and sixth petitions—the will of God, and the deliverance from all evil—to God the Sanctifier and Finisher (the Holy Ghost).

PART SECOND.

The Christian Faith.

XII. Of the Christian Faith.

1. *What is Christian faith?*

CHRISTIAN faith is trust in Christ as our Lord and Saviour, whereby we become partakers of his life and all his benefits.

* John 6, 47. Verily, verily, I say unto you, He that believeth on me, hath everlasting life.

* Gal. 2, 20. I live; yet not I, but Christ liveth in me: and the life which I now live in the flesh, I live by the faith of the Son of God, who loved me and gave himself for me.

2. *What belongs to true faith?*

A knowledge of God and of Christ, a belief in his word, and a hearty confidence in his mercy.

(1.) *Knowledge:* Heb. 11, 6. He that cometh to God must believe that he is, and that he is a rewarder of them that diligently seek him.—John 17, 3. This is life eternal, that they might know thee the only true God, and Jesus Christ whom thou hast sent.—John 6, 69. We believe and are sure, etc. —2 Tim. 1, 12. I know whom I have believed, and am persuaded, etc.

(2.) *Belief* in the word of God and assent to it: Acts 24, 14. I worship the God of my fathers, believing all things which are written in the law and in the prophets.—1 Thess. 2, 13. When ye received the word of God [the gospel] which ye heard of us, ye received it not as the word of men, but (as it is in truth) the word of God, which effectually worketh also in you that believe.

(3.) *Confidence* and *trust:* * Heb. 11, 1. Faith is the substance [or, assurance] of things hoped for, the evidence [or, conviction] of things not seen.—Heb. 10, 22. Let us draw near with a true heart in full assurance of faith.

Examples: Abraham, the father of the faithful (comp. Rom. 4, 20, 21), and the whole cloud of witnesses, Heb. 11 and 12.

OF THE CHRISTIAN FAITH. 41

3. *What is the object of faith?*

The triune God and his holy word, especially the gospel of Christ.

* Mark 1, 15. Repent ye, and believe the gospel.
Acts 16, 31. Believe on the Lord Jesus Christ.
John 3, 16. 36; 6, 47; 1 John 5, 10.

4. *Who works faith in us?*

The Holy Spirit.

* 1 Cor. 12, 3. No man can say that Jesus is the Lord, but by the Holy Ghost.
Gal. 5, 22. The fruit of the Spirit is ... faith.
Matt. 16, 17; John 15, 26; 2 Cor. 3, 5.

5. *How does the Holy Spirit work faith?*

By the means of grace, especially the preaching of the gospel and study of his word.

* Rom. 10, 17. Faith cometh by hearing [or, preaching], and hearing by the word of God.
John 17, 20 (which shall believe on me through their word); 1 Pet. 1, 23 (being born again ... by the word of God); James 1, 18.

6. *What is the effect of faith?*

Faith justifies and saves.

* Rom. 10, 10. With the heart man believeth unto righteousness; and with the mouth confession is made unto salvation.—Comp. 3, 24; 5, 1; Gal. 2, 20; Phil. 3, 8. 9.
* Mark 16, 16. He that believeth and is baptized shall be saved; but he that believeth not shall be damned.
Eph. 2, 8. 9. By grace are ye saved, through faith.
Acts 16. 31. Believe on the Lord Jesus Christ, and thou shalt be saved, and thy house.
John 3, 16. 36; Acts 15, 11; 1 John 5, 10.

7. *Is faith then the ground or cause of salvation?*

No; Jesus Christ is the only ground of our salvation.

* Acts 4, 12. Neither is there salvation in any other: for there is none other name under heaven given among men, whereby we must be saved.
Acts 15, 11· Eph. 2, 8. 9; 1 Tim 2, 5. 6.

8. *What, then, has faith to do with salvation?*

It is the condition of salvation, because it accepts and appropriates Jesus Christ and his merits to our personal benefit.

John 6, 47. He that believeth on me hath everlasting life.
* Heb. 11, 6. Without faith it is impossible to please God; for he that cometh to God must believe that he is, and that he is a rewarder of them that diligently seek him.

9. *What is the nature of justifying and saving faith?*

It must be living, and bring forth good works.

* Matt. 7, 17. 20. Every good tree bringeth forth good fruit; but a corrupt tree bringeth forth evil fruit. ... Wherefore by their fruits ye shall know them.
* Gal. 5, 6. In Jesus Christ neither circumcision [*i.e.* Jewish descent] availeth any thing, nor uncircumcision [gentile descent]: but faith, which worketh by love.

10. *Is there also a dead faith?*

Yes; the devils also believe and tremble.

1 Cor. 13, 2. Though I have all faith, so that I could remove mountains, and have not charity, I am nothing.
* James 2, 26. As the body without the spirit is dead, so faith without works is dead also.
James 2, 19. 20.

11. *Should we also confess our faith?*

Yes; we should openly confess Christ before men, and never be ashamed of him.

* Matt. 10, 32. 33. Whosoever shall confess me before men, him will I confess also before my Father which is in heaven. But whosoever shall deny me before men, him will I also deny before my Father which is in heaven.
* Rom. 10, 10. With the heart man believeth unto righteousness; and with the mouth confession is made unto salvation.
Rom. 1, 16. I am not ashamed of the gospel of Christ.

Notes.

This lesson refers to the faith *by which* we believe (*subjective* faith, fides *qua credimus*), the following lessons, to the faith *which* we believe, or the contents and object of faith (*objective* faith, Creed, fides *quæ creditur*.)

Q. 8. Faith has no more merit on this account in the eyes of God than the taking of the medicine by the sick, or the seizing of the hand of the deliverer by a drowning man.

XIII. The Apostles' Creed.

1. What is the Apostles' Creed?

A summary of the chief articles of the Christian faith which are necessary to our salvation.

2. Why is it called the Apostles' Creed?

Because it agrees with the doctrine of the apostles.

3. Repeat this Creed.

1. What do you believe concerning God the Father?

I believe in God the Father Almighty, Maker of heaven and earth.

2. What is God?

God is a spirit, infinite, eternal, personal, and unchangeable in his being, wisdom, power, holiness, justice, goodness, and truth.*

* John 4, 24. God is a Spirit.
* 1 John 4, 8. God is love.
1 John 1, 5. God is light, and in him is no darkness at all.
* Rom. 11, 36. Of him, and through him, and to him, are all things.
1 Tim. 1, 17; 6, 15. 16; James 1, 17; Rev. 4, 8; Ex. 3, 14; Job 11, 7–9; Ps. 36, 9; John 5, 26.

3. Whence do you know the existence of God?

From the works of creation, the conscience of man, the history of the world, and from the

4. How is the Creed divided?

Into three parts, which correspond to the three persons of the Holy Trinity.

5. Of what does the first part treat?

Of God the Father, and our creation.

* The place of departed spirits.

6. *Of what does the second part treat?*

Of God the Son, and our redemption.

7. *Of what does the third part treat?*

Of God the Holy Ghost, and our sanctification.

8. *Why do you say: I believe?*

Because I must believe for myself, and become personally united to Christ, in order to be saved.

but a corrupt tree bringeth forth evil fruit.... Wherefore by their fruits ye shall know them.

* Gal. 5, 6. In Jesus Christ neither circumcision [*i.e.* Jewish descent] availeth any thing, nor uncircumcision [gentile descent]: but faith, which worketh by love.

10. *Is there also a dead faith?*

Yes; the devils also believe and tremble.

1 Cor. 13, 2. Though I have all faith, so that I could remove mountains, and have not charity, I am nothing.

* James 2, 26. As the body without the spirit is dead, so faith without works is dead also.

James 2, 19. 20.

11. *Should we also confess our faith?*

Yes; we should openly confess Christ before men, and never be ashamed of him.

* Matt. 10, 32. 33. Whosoever shall confess me before men, him will I confess also before my Father which is in heaven. But whosoever shall deny me before men, him will I also deny before my Father which is in heaven.

* Rom. 10, 10. With the heart man believeth unto rightPrayer. It is the model confession of faith, ever old and ever new, and can never be superseded.

Q. 3. *Hades*, i.e. *the region of the dead,* or *the underworld* (the Hebrew *sheol*), is the proper word, which should have been retained, like so many other Greek terms in our English Bible (as *Christ, Bible, baptism, apostle, angel,* etc.), instead of *hell,* which is apt to mislead. For in modern usage *hell* (probably from the Saxon word *helan,* to *cover,* to *conceal*) signifies the state and place of *eternal damnation,* like the Hebrew *gehenna* (which occurs twelve times in the Greek Testament); while *hades* (which occurs eleven times in the Greek Testament, and is likewise translated *hell* in the Common Version, except in 1 Cor. 15, 55) is the abode of *all* the departed, both the righteous and wicked, and corresponds to the Hebrew *sheol*. The American editions of the *Book of Common Prayer* leave it optional with the minister to use in the Creed *hell*, or *the place of departed spirits*, or to omit the clause altogether. The Common Prayer Book places a (,) after *hell*, and thus connects the descent into hades with the resurrection in one article, while others, on the contrary, connect it with the preceding article by placing a (,) after *buried*. It forms rather a separate article, and should be included in (;), as above.

Q. 4. The *parts* are marked by paragraphs; the several *articles* by (:), giving one article to the first, eight articles to the second, and four articles to the third part. Some, however, distinguish fourteen, others only twelve articles. Hence also the difference in punctuation.

XIV. The Existence and Attributes of God.

1. *What do you believe concerning God the Father?*

I believe in God the Father Almighty, Maker of heaven and earth.

2. *What is God?*

God is a spirit, infinite, eternal, personal, and unchangeable in his being, wisdom, power, holiness, justice, goodness, and truth.*

* John 4, 24. God is a Spirit.
* 1 John 4, 8. God is love.
1 John 1, 5. God is light, and in him is no darkness at all.
* Rom. 11, 36. Of him, and through him, and to him, are all things.
1 Tim. 1, 17; 6, 15. 16; James 1, 17; Rev. 4, 8; Ex. 3, 14; Job 11, 7–9; Ps. 36, 9; John 5, 26.

3. *Whence do you know the existence of God?*

From the works of creation, the conscience of man, the history of the world, and from the Holy Scripture.

Ps. 19, 2–4; Rom. 1, 19. 20; Rom. 2, 14. 15; Acts 14, 17; 17, 27. 28; John 1, 18; 2 Tim. 3, 16. 17; Heb. 1, 1. 2; 2 Pet. 1, 19. Comp. Less. III. Q. 1.

* Westminster Assembly's definition, with the word "personal" added.

4. *Are there any reasonable men who deny the existence of God?*

No; only the fool says in his heart: There is no God.

Ps. 14, 1.

5. *What are the principal attributes of God?*

God is eternal, almighty, omnipresent, omniscient, most wise, holy, righteous, longsuffering, and full of love, mercy, and truth.

Ex. 34, 6. The Lord God is merciful and gracious, longsuffering, and abundant in goodness and truth.

1 Tim. 1, 17. Now unto the King eternal, immortal, invisible, the only wise God, be honor and glory for ever and ever. Comp. 1 Tim. 6, 15. 16.

NOTES AND HINTS.

Q. 1. The Scriptures represent God as *Life, Spirit, Light, Love,* and *Truth,* i.e. as the personal fulness and independent source of all life, spirit, light, love, and truth. The creature *has* life, but God *is* Life. God is infinitely greater than our sublimest conceptions of him.

Q. 4. Although there are few *theoretical* atheists, there are, alas! everywhere many *practical* atheists, who live as if there were no God and no eternity. And then there are false theories of God, as *dualism, polytheism, deism,* and *pantheism.* The Bible reveals to us the only true and living God, Father, Son, and Holy Ghost. All other gods are mere idols or empty fancies.

Q. 5. The passages on the several *attributes* or *perfections* of God are too numerous to be quoted in full. The attributes may be divided into: (1) *metaphysical,* which relate to the nature or general being of God, as eternity, almightiness, omnipresence, unchangeableness; (2) *intellectual,* or attributes of the divine mind, as wisdom, omniscience; (3) *moral,* or attributes of the divine will: holiness, righteousness, longsuffering, goodness, kindness, love, mercy, and faithfulness.

The teacher may explain the principal attributes in a popular manner and select the principal passages for each, as follows: God is *eternal;* i.e. he has neither beginning nor end, 1 Tim. 1, 7; Ps. 90, 2–4; 102, 27. God is *almighty;* i.e. he can create at pleasure, or, with him nothing is impossible (except sin and all that is inconsistent with his character), Isa. 32, 17; Ps. 115, 3; Luke 1, 37; Matt. 19, 26. God is *omnipresent;* i.e. he is everywhere, and fills all things with his power. Ps. 139, 7–12; 1 Kings 8, 27; Jer. 23, 23. 24. God is *omniscient;* i.e. he knows all things, and knows them perfectly, Ps. 139, 1–6. God is *holy;* i.e. free from all sin and evil, and morally perfect, Ps. 5, 4; Isa. 6, 3; Rev. 4, 8. God is *righteous;* i.e. he rewards the good and punishes the wicked, Ex. 34, 7; Ps. 5, 5. 6; Rom. 1, 18; 2, 6–11. God is *patient* and *longsuffering;* i.e. he delays the righteous punishment of the sinner, and gives him time to repent, Ex. 34, 6. 7; Ps. 103, 8. God is *love;* i.e. he communicates himself to his creatures, and makes them partakers of his glory and bliss. Love is the deepest and most comprehensive attribute of God, the animating soul and uniting bond of all his perfections: hence God is called *love*, *i. e.* pure love, absolute love, love itself, 1 John 4, 8. *Mercy* is *redeeming* love, or love as revealed in Christ in the salvation of sinners.

XV. The Unity and Trinity of God.

1. *Are there more Gods than one?*

There is but one living and true God.

Ex. 20, 2. 3. I am the Lord thy God.... Thou shalt have no other gods before me.

* Deut. 6, 4. Hear, O Israel: The Lord our God is one Lord.

Isa. 44, 6. I am the first, and I am the last, and beside me there is no God.

John 17, 3. This is life eternal, that they might know thee the only true God, and Jesus Christ whom thou hast sent.

1 Cor. 8, 4. There is none other God but one.

1 Cor. 8, 6. To us there is but one God, the Father, of whom are all things, and we in him; and one Lord Jesus Christ, by whom are all things, and we by him.

1 Thess. 1, 9. Ye turned to God from idols to serve the living and true God.

1 John 5, 21. Little children, keep yourselves from idols.

2. *How is God triune, and yet one?*

God is triune in person, but one in essence.

3. *Name the three persons in the one Divine being.*

The Father, the Son, and the Holy Ghost; and these three are one.

* Matt. 28, 19. Go ye, therefore, and teach all nations, baptizing them in the name of the Father, and of the Son, and of the Holy Ghost.

* 2 Cor. 13, 13. The grace of the Lord Jesus Christ, and the love of God [the Father], and the communion of the Holy Ghost, be with you all.

Comp. Matt. 3, 16. 17 (where the Father, the Son, and the Holy Spirit in the form of a descending dove, are distinguished at the baptism of Christ); John 14, 16; 1 Pet. 1, 2; Rev. 1, 4. 5; also the intimations of the Old Testament, in the account of creation, Gen. 1, 1–3, where *God* creates through the *Word*, *i.e.* Christ according to his divine nature (comp. Ps. 33, 3; John 1,

1. 3; Heb. 1, 2), and where the *Spirit* of God moves upon the face of the waters; the *threefold blessing* of Aaron, Num. 6, 24 –26 (comp. with the apostolic benediction, 2 Cor. 13, 13); and the *thrice holy* of the Seraphim, Isa 6, 3.

4. *Why do you believe in the Holy Trinity?*

Because God has so revealed himself in his word, and continues so to reveal himself.

5. *How does God reveal himself?*

As Father in the work of creation, as Son in the work of redemption, and as Holy Spirit in the work of sanctification.

NOTES AND HINTS.

Q. 3. The Scripture proof for the doctrine of the Holy Trinity rests not simply on the express passages above quoted, but on all those passages which teach the divinity of Christ or of the Holy Spirit separately. (Comp. Less. XXIV. and XXXIII.) For the divinity of Christ and the Holy Spirit cannot be held in connection with the fundamental doctrine of the *unity* of the Godhead, except in the form of *tri-unity* or *trinity*, i.e. the unity of essence and the trinity of persons. Finally, the trinity follows from the whole revelation of God in the threefold work of creation, redemption, and sanctification. Hence it is the most comprehensive doctrine, and the holy symbol of the Christian religion as distinct from heathen polytheism on the one hand, and the abstract and lifeless monotheism of the Jews and Mohammedans on the other.

Q. 5. God is essentially triune from eternity: the Father neither begotten nor proceeding, the Son eternally begotten of the substance of the Father and beloved by the Father, the Holy Ghost eternally proceeding from the Father and the Son and uniting both. But he has also revealed himself as such, and it is from the trinity of revelation that we infer the trinity of being or essence. Each person has his peculiar work, yet all co-operate together in every stage of revelation. Thus, God the Father creates and preserves the world, but through his Son, in the Holy Spirit. Christ redeems the world, but as sent by the Father and filled with the Holy Spirit. The Holy Spirit regenerates and sanctifies, but he proceeds from the Father and the Son, and applies the work of the Son.

The Holy Trinity is more an object of adoration than of speculation. Still, it may be brought somewhat nearer to our comprehension by analogies, such as the trinity of the human being—body, soul, and spirit; the trinity of the mental faculties—cognition, volition, and feeling; the three grammatical persons—I, thou, he; the trinity of love—the loving subject, the beloved object, and the union of both (hence the saying of Augustin: "Where there is love there is trinity"); the threefold nature of self-consciousness, etc. Only we must not suppose that any of these analogies borrowed from the creature are more than very imperfect illustrations of the deepest and most unfathomable mystery of the Christian faith.

XVI. The Creation of the World.

1. *Who created the world?*

God the Father Almighty.

* Gen. 1, 1. In the beginning God created the heaven and the earth.

Ex. 20, 11. In six days the Lord made heaven and earth, the sea, and all that in them is.

Comp. the two accounts of creation, Gen. 1 and 2; also Ps. 33, 6; 102, 25; Neh. 9, 6; Heb. 1, 10; 3, 4; 11, 3.

2. *What do you mean by the world which God made?*

Heaven and earth, and all that in them is, things visible and invisible, men and angels.

Ex. 20, 11; Col. 1, 16.

3. *Through whom did God create the world?*

Through his Son, the eternal Word.

* Ps. 33, 6. By the Word of the Lord were the heavens made; and all the host of them by the breath [spirit] of his mouth.

John 1, 3. All things were made by him [*i.e.* the Logos or eternal Word, which was in the beginning, v. 1, and which in the fulness of time was made flesh, v. 14]; and without him was not any thing made that was made.

Col. 1, 15. By him [Christ] were all things created, that are in heaven and that are in earth, visible and invisible, whether they be thrones, or principalities, or powers; all things were created by him, and for him.

Gen. 1, 3 (God spake: Let there be light); Heb. 1, 2; 1 Cor. 8, 6.

4. *When did God create the world?*

In the beginning.

Gen. 1, 1; Ps. 102, 5.

5. *Of what did God create the world?*

Out of nothing, by his almighty will.

* Heb. 11, 3. Through faith we understand that the world

were framed by the word of God, so that things which are seen were not made of things which do appear.

Ps. 33, 6-9; Rom. 4, 17; Rev. 4, 11.

6. *How was the world when God made it?*

Very good.

* Gen. 1, 31. God saw every thing that he had made, and behold, it was very good.

7. *For what end did God create the world?*

For his own glory, and for the happiness of his creatures.

* Rom. 11, 36. Of him, and through him, and to him, are all things: to whom be glory forever.

Prov. 16, 4. The Lord hath made all things for himself.

Ps. 145, 10. All thy works shall praise thee, O Lord; and thy saints shall bless thee.

* Rom. 14, 8. Whether we live, we live unto the Lord; and whether we die, we die unto the Lord: whether we live, therefore, or die, we are the Lord's.

8. *What does the article on creation teach you?*

That in all the works of creation I should admire and adore the infinite majesty, power, wisdom, and goodness of God.

* Ps. 19, 1. The heavens declare the glory of God; and the firmament showeth his handywork.

* Ps. 104, 24. O Lord, how manifold are thy works! In wisdom hast thou made them all: the earth is full of thy riches.

NOTES AND HINTS.

Q. 1. To *create*, means, strictly speaking, to bring forth something out of nothing, or to call things from non-existence into existence. In this sense God alone can create; while men can only produce something new out of material already existing. There is, moreover, a difference between *creation* and *generation*. The *world* was *created* of nothing, by the free *will* of God, and is different from him in substance; the *Son* is *begotten* from eternity, of the *substance* of the Father, and is co-equal, or of the same substance, with him.

Q. 4. Before the creation there was no *time*, but only the *eternal* God, who created time, and fills it, as he fills space, but without being subject to its limits or divisions. The world, then, was not made *in time*, but *together with time;* time and space being part of the world, or the forms under which it exists.

Q. 5. The formula *out of nothing* is derived from 2 Mac. 7, 28 (*ex nihilo*, in the Latin Bible), and is negative, denying the pre-existence of matter. It must be completed by the positive formula, that God created all things *by his almighty will*, which is the only and all-sufficient cause of creation.

Q. 7. More accurately expressed the answer should read: *For his own glory, through the happiness of his creatures.* There can be but *one* ultimate end of the creation, and this is the *glory of God*, which, however, implies the *happiness* of his children. The Westminster Catechism, in the first question on the *chief end of man*, combines the two in the well chosen answer: *to glorify God and to enjoy him forever.* The true happiness of man is to glorify God.

XVII. Preservation and Providence.

1. *What do you mean by the preservation of the world?*

That God, by his almighty and omnipresent power, keeps the world in existence, and, by his goodness, provides all his creatures with food, raiment, and shelter.

* Ps. 23, 1. 2. The Lord is my shepherd, I shall not want. He maketh me to lie down in green pastures: he leadeth me beside the still waters.

* Ps. 145, 15. 16. The eyes of all wait upon thee [or, look unto thee]; and thou givest them their meat in due season. Thou openest thine hand, and satisfiest the desire of every living thing.

* Acts 17, 28. In him we live, and move, and have our being.

Isa. 49, 15. 16. Can a woman forget her sucking child, that she should not have compassion on the son of her womb? Yea, they may forget, yet will I not forget thee. Behold, I have graven thee upon the palms of my hands.

Ps. 103, 13; 104, 27. 28; 147, 9; John 5, 17; Col. 1, 17; Heb. 1, 3 ("upholding all things by the word of his power"); Acts 17, 25. 26.

2. *Does God Almighty care even for the smallest of his creatures?*

God cares even for the fowls of the air, and the lilies of the field: how much more, then, for man, who was made in God's image.

* Matt. 6, 26. Behold the fowls of the air: for they sow not, neither do they reap, nor gather into barns; yet your heavenly Father feedeth them.

Matt. 6, 28–31. Consider the lilies of the field, how they grow; they toil not, neither do they spin [like men in providing for their raiment]: and yet I say unto you, that even Solomon in all his glory was not arrayed like one of these. Wherefore, if God so clothe the grass of the field, which to-day is, and to-morrow is cast into the oven, shall he not much more clothe you, O ye of little faith?

3. *What do you mean by the providence of God and the government of the world?*

That God rules the world according to an eternal plan of infinite wisdom and love, and causes all things, even sin and evil, to work together for the glory of his name and the welfare of his children.

* Rom. 8, 28. We know that all things work together for good to them that love God, to them who are the called according to his purpose.

Gen. 50, 20. As for you, ye thought evil against me; but God meant it unto good. [Words of Joseph to his brothers, who sold him into Egypt, where God made him a mighty lord.]

* Ps. 76, 10. Surely the wrath of man shall praise thee: the remainder of wrath shalt thou restrain.

Ps. 91, 10–14; Prov. 2, 7. 8; Job 5, 19.

Examples of the overruling providence of God in making good to come out of evil: The history of Joseph (Gen. 50); Pharaoh and the deliverance of Israel (Ex. 9, 16); Satan and Job; the treason of Judas and the atoning death of Christ.

4. *Is there, then, no such thing as chance?*

No: all things come from the wise and fatherly will of God; seed-time and harvest, heat and cold, summer and winter, day and night, wealth and poverty, health and sickness, life and death.

* Matt. 10, 29–31. Are not two sparrows sold for a farthing? and one of them shall not fall on the ground without your Father. But the very hairs of your head are all numbered. Fear ye not, therefore; ye are of more value than many sparrows.

Luke 12, 7; 21, 18; Matt. 6, 26–31; Gen. 8, 22; Ps. 139, 16

5. *What should the belief in Providence teach you?*

To be thankful in prosperity, patient in adversity, and at all times to put my trust in God, who does all things well.

* 1 Thess. 5, 18. In every thing give thanks.

Ps. 118, 1. O give thanks unto the Lord; for he is good: because his mercy endureth forever.

Ps. 73, 25. 26. Whom have I in heaven but thee? and there is none upon earth that I desire beside thee. My flesh and my heart faileth: but God is the strength of my heart, and my portion forever.

Ps. 37, 5. Commit thy way unto the Lord; trust also in him; and he shall bring it to pass.

1 Pet. 3, 7. Cast all your care upon God; for he careth for you.

* Rom. 8, 38. 39. I am persuaded, that neither death, nor life, nor angels, nor principalities, nor powers, nor things present, nor things to come, nor height, nor depth, nor any other creature, shall be able to separate us from the love of God, which is in Christ Jesus our Lord.

NOTES AND HINTS.

Q. 4. What men call *accidents*, are God's appointed *incidents*. Shakespeare says:

"There's a Divinity that shapes our ends,
Rough hew them how we will."

XVIII. The State of Innocence.

1. *What is man?*

Man is a rational and immortal being in a material body.

* Gen. 2, 7. The Lord God formed man of the dust of the ground, and breathed into his nostrils the breath of life; and man became a living soul.

Eccles. 12, 7. Then shall the dust return to the earth as it was; and the spirit shall return unto God who gave it.

Matt. 10, 28. Fear not them which kill the body, but are not able to kill the soul; but rather fear him which is able to destroy both soul and body in hell.

1 Thess. 5, 23. The very God of peace sanctify you wholly; and I pray God your whole spirit, and soul, and body be preserved blameless unto the coming of our Lord Jesus Christ.

2. *How did God create man?*

God created man in his own image.

* Gen. 1, 27: God created man in his own image, in the image of God created he him; male and female created he them.

* Ps. 139, 14. I will praise thee; for I am fearfully and wonderfully made.

Comp. Gen. 5, 1 (in the likeness of God made he him); 9, 6 (in the image of God made he man); 1 Cor. 11, 7 (man is the image and glory of God); James 3, 9 (men...made after the similitude of God); Eccles. 7, 29 (God made man upright).

3. *What does this mean?*

God made man good and holy, gave him dominion over nature, and endowed him with all the faculties for intellectual and moral perfection.

* Gen. 1, 31. And God saw every thing that he had made, and, behold, it was very good.

Gen. 1, 26. And God said, Let us make man in our image, after our likeness: and let them have dominion over the fish of the sea, and over the fowl of the air, and over the cattle, and over all the earth, and over every creeping thing that creepeth upon the earth.—Comp. v. 28; 9, 2; Ps. 8, 7–9.

Eph. 4, 24. Put on the new man, which after God is created in righteousness and true holiness. [This refers to the *renewal* of the image of God by the regeneration of the Spirit.]

4. *What is the original state of man called?*

The state of innocence.

5. *Why so?*

Because man was free from sin, and knew no sin.

6. *Who were our first parents?*

Adam and Eve.

7. *Where did they live in the state of innocence?*

In paradise, in blessed communion with God.
Gen. 2, 8.

8. *Are there other rational beings besides men?*

Yes: the angels.

9. *What are the angels?*

Holy and blessed spirits in heaven who serve God, and rejoice in the salvation of sinners.

* Heb. 1, 14. Are they not all ministering spirits, sent forth to minister for them who shall be heirs of salvation?

Luke 15, 10. There is joy in the presence of the angels of God over one sinner that repenteth.

Matt. 18, 10. Take heed that ye despise not one of these little ones; for I say unto you, That in heaven their angels do always behold the face of my Father which is in heaven.

Ps. 103, 20. Bless the Lord, ye his angels, that excel in strength, that do his commandments, hearkening unto the voice of his word.

Job 38, 7. When the morning stars sang together, and all the sons of God [angels] shouted for joy.

The angels at the birth of Christ, Luke 2, 8–14: in the agony of Gethsemane. 22, 43; on the resurrection-morning, 24, 23; at the ascension, Acts 1, 10. 11; at the principal stages of the history of the church, Acts 5, 19; 12, 7. 9–10. 15; 8, 26; 10, 3. 7. 22; 27, 23; Rev. 5, 2; 7, 1. 2. 11; 8, 2, etc.; and at the final coming of Christ to judge the world, Matt. 25, 31.

10. *Did all angels remain holy?*

No: some fell from their first estate, and were cast out of heaven.

John 8, 44. He [the devil] abode not in the truth.

2 Pet. 2, 4. God spared not the angels that sinned, but cast them down to hell, and delivered them into chains of darkness, to be reserved unto judgment.

Jude 6. The angels which kept not their first estate, but left their own habitation, he hath reserved in everlasting chains, under darkness, unto the judgment of the great day.

Matt. 25, 41. Depart from me, ye cursed, into everlasting fire, prepared for the devil and his angels.

NOTES AND HINTS.

Q. 3. The holiness and perfection of Adam *before the fall* must not be confounded with the holiness and perfection of the redeemed *after the resurrection.* They differ from each other as the germ from the fruit, as childhood from manhood, as innocence from confirmed virtue, as the possibility of not sinning from the impossibility of sinning. Adam's holiness needed trial and temptation, and was subject to fall; the holiness after the resurrection is the victory over all temptation and sin, and can never be lost. So, also, the immortality of the body of Adam was conditional only (a possibility not to die), and liable to be lost by yielding to temptation; while the immortality of the resurrection-body is absolute (an impossibility to die), and can never give way to a second death. Consequently, the redemption of Christ is far more than a mere recovery of the state of paradise; the gain of the second Adam, who is "the Lord from heaven," is far greater than the loss of the first Adam, who was "of the earth, earthy."—Comp. the "*much more*" in Rom. 5, 17. 20; and 1 Cor. 15, 45–49.

Q. 4. There are three states or conditions in the moral history of man: (1.) the state of innocence; (2.) the state of sin and death; (3.) the state of redemption and holiness.

Q. 5. The innocence of *Adam* and *Eve* before the fall excludes all sin and moral defect, and includes a conscious communion with God: the Innocence of *children* after the fall is relative, and consists simply in the *ignorance* of sin and the absence of *actual* transgression.

Q. 9. The angels are *rational*, or intelligent and moral beings, like men, but without a *material* body, without sex (Matt. 22, 30), and, consequently, they do not propagate themselves, like men, but were probably all created at the same time. They are superior to man in his *present* state, both in intelligence and in holiness; but the *ultimate* destiny of man seems to be higher, on account of the incarnation and the *permanent* assumption of the *human* nature into personal union with the *divine* in Christ (comp. Heb. 2, 16).

Q. 10. The *fall of angels* must have taken place *before* the fall of man, and, in all probability, before his creation; for Adam fell by the temptation of Satan, a fallen angel. Beyond this the Bible does not inform us as to the *time* of their creation. Some divines suppose that the angels were created on the first day, together with the light; others, that they were created before the material universe, and that their moral fall produced the material chaos (Gen. 1, 2), out of which God created the *present* world, or "heaven and earth." The last is also Milton's view in his magnificent picture of Satan's revolt in the first book of "Paradise Lost." But all this, of course, is pious speculation or fancy, and not matter of doctrine.

XIX. The Fall.

1. *Did our first parents remain in the state of innocence?*

No: they fell, and became sinners.

2. *Wherein did the fall consist?*

In disobedience to God.

Gen. 3, 6.

THE FALL.

3. *What had God commanded them?*
Not to eat of the tree of the knowledge of good and evil.

Gen. 3, 16. 17. Of every tree of the garden thou mayest freely eat: but of the tree of the knowledge of good and evil, thou shalt not eat of it; for in the day that thou eatest thereof hou shalt surely die.—Comp. Gen. 3, 3.

4. *Why did God give them this commandment?*
In order to exercise them in obedience, and to confirm them in goodness.

5. *What were the stages of the fall?*
First, doubt of the word of God; then, pride and lust; and finally, the actual transgression by eating of the forbidden fruit.

Gen. 3, 3-6.

6. *Who tempted Adam and Eve to sin?*
The devil, in the disguise of a serpent.

Gen. 3, 4. And the serpent said unto the woman; Ye shall not surely die.
John 8, 44. The devil was a murderer from the beginning. [For sin, which he introduced, is first a murder of the soul, and then also, of the body, being the cause of death.]
2 Cor. 11, 3. The serpent beguiled Eve through his subtilty.
Rev. 12, 9. The great dragon was cast out, that old serpent, called the Devil, and Satan, which deceiveth the whole world.
—Comp. 20, 2. (Comp. Wisd. of Sol. 2, 24. Through envy of the devil came death into the world.)

7. *Who is the devil?*
The chief of the fallen angels, and the prince of darkness.

John 8, 44. The devil was a murderer from the beginning, and abode not in the truth [consequently, he was once in the truth, but fell from his original state], because there is no truth in him. When he speaketh a lie, he speaketh of his own: for he is a liar, and the father of it.

Eph. 6, 11. 12. Put on the whole armor of God, that ye may be able to stand against the wiles of the devil. For we wrestle not against flesh and blood, but against principalities, against powers, against the rulers of the darkness of this world, against spiritual wickedness [or, wicked spirits] in high places.

James 4, 7. Resist the devil, and he will flee from you.

Comp. Job 1, 7; 2, 2; Matt. 9, 34; 12, 24-27; 13, 19. 39; 1 Pet. 5, 8. 9; 2 Pet. 2, 4; Jude 6; Rev. 12, 12; 20, 9.

Satan (from the Hebrew) means adversary, persecutor; *devil* (from the Greek) means accuser, slanderer, traducer.

8. *Was the fall of man necessary?*

No: man might and ought to have resisted the temptation, as the good angels did in heaven, and as Jesus did in the wilderness.

9. *What were the consequences of the fall?*

Death, and expulsion from paradise.

Gen. 3, 14-19. 24; Rom. 5, 12; 6, 23; James 1, 15; 1 Cor. 15, 21. 22.

10. *What is death?*

All temporal and eternal evil, but more particularly the extinction of physical life.

11. *Was the fall of man confined to our first parents?*

No: sin and death passed upon all the descendants of Adam.

* Rom. 5, 12. By one man sin entered into the world, and death by sin; and so death passed upon all men, for that all have sinned.—Comp. 1 Cor. 15, 21. 22.

Rom. 11, 32. God hath concluded them all in unbelief, that he might have mercy upon all.—Comp. Gal. 3, 22.

12. *Is there, then, no human being without sin?*

Not one, except only Jesus Christ, who redeemed us from sin.

* Rom. 3, 23. All have sinned, and come short of the glory of God.—Comp. v. 9-12.

* 1 John 1, 8. If we say that we have no sin, we deceive ourselves, and the truth is not in us.

Job 15, 14–16. What is man, that he should be clean? and he which is born of a woman, that he should be righteous? Behold, he putteth no trust in his saints; yea, the heavens are not clean in his sight. How much more abominable and filthy is man, which drinketh iniquity like water?

Eccles. 7, 20. There is not a just man upon earth, that doeth good and sinneth not.

Isa. 53, 6. All we like sheep have gone astray; we have turned every one to his own way; and the Lord hath laid on him the iniquity of us all.

Prov. 20, 9; 1 Kings 8, 46 ("there is no man that sinneth not"); 2 Chron. 6, 36; James 3, 2.

Heb. 4, 15. He [Christ] was in all points tempted like as we are, yet without sin.

Notes and Hints.

Q. 1–4. The history of the temptation and fall of Adam and Eve applies at the same time to their whole posterity, or to human nature, which they represent. It is, therefore, of universal significance, and repeats itself in daily experience. The account in Genesis, whatever be its difficulties as to a literal explanation, proves its divine origin by its intrinsic truthfulness and exact conformity to the nature and progress of sin.

Q. 5. The fall commenced inwardly in the heart, and then completed itself in the outward act. Its progress was this: (1.) *Unbelief*, or doubt concerning the truth of God's commandment, suggested by the insidious lie of the father of lies: "Ye shall not surely die," Gen. 3, 4. (2.) *Pride*, or desire to be like God in the false sense of independence of him: "Ye shall be as God, knowing good and evil." (3.) *Concupiscence*, or sensual desire in the form of the lust of the eye: "The woman saw that the tree was good for food, and that it was pleasant to the eyes, and a tree to be desired." (4.) The actual *deed:* "She took the fruit thereof, and did eat." (5.) The *seduction* by evil example: "And she gave unto her husband with her; and he did eat."

Q. 6, 7. The temptation of Satan does not destroy the guilt of man, yet redemption is made easier; the seduced party being always less guilty than the seducer. Nevertheless, every man must feel sin as *his own personal* guilt, and cannot feel it too deeply. The doctrine of Satan should not weaken, but strengthen and deepen, the sense of the terrible power and extent of sin, and put us the more on our guard against temptation. Eph. 6, 11. 12; 1 Pet. 5, 8. 9.

Q. 8. Examples of a successful resistance to temptation are furnished by the good angels who kept their first estate (Jude 6), and by Christ when tempted by the devil in the wilderness (Matt. 4, 1–11). Temptation or trial was necessary to confirm our first parents, but obedience to temptation was their own free voluntary act. God could not prevent it without interfering with the freedom and moral accountability of man, whom he created a freeman, not a slave. But God, of course, foresaw the fall from eternity, and permitted it as a means or occasion for greater good, or in view of the highest manifestation of his infinite love and mercy in the plan of redemption. He allowed sin to abound by the guilt of the first Adam, in order that grace might much more abound by the merit of the second Adam (Rom. 5, 20). "He concluded them all in unbelief, that he might have mercy upon all" (Rom. 11, 32; Gal. 3, 11). So far we may go in this most difficult problem, and exclaim, with St. Paul: "O the depth of the riches both of the wisdom and knowledge of God!" (Rom. 11, 33). What lies beyond is theological speculation and transcendental mystery.

Q. 10. The threat of God, Gen. 2, 17, "In the day that thou eatest thereof thou shalt surely die," is not to be understood of physical death only,—for Adam and Eve lived many years after the fall,—but in a wider sense, which comprehends physical death as an ultimate result. Our first parents, the moment they transgressed the divine commandment, became mortal, or began to die, first spiritually and then physically. Spiritual death culminates in eternal misery, temporal death in the extinction of physical life.

Q. 12. The passages quoted under this question leave no room for the recent Roman Catholic dogma, proclaimed in 1854, of the sinlessness of the Virgin Mary. Although the blessed mother of the Redeemer, she herself stood in need of redemption, and was purged from sin and guilt by the blood of Christ.

XX. Of Sin.

1. *What is sin?*

The transgression of the law of God.

* 1 John 3, 4. Whosoever committeth sin, transgresseth also the law: for sin is the transgression of the law.
Rom. 4, 15; 5, 13.

2. *Whence do you know sin?*

From the natural law of conscience, but more fully from the revealed law of God.

* Rom. 3, 20. By the law is the knowledge of sin.
Rom. 7, 7. I had not known sin but by the law: for I had not known lust except the law had said, Thou shalt not covet.
Rom. 2, 14. 15 (their conscience also bearing witness); John 8, 9 (being convicted by their own conscience).
EXAMPLES of the power of conscience: Adam, Gen. 3, 7-11; Cain, Gen. 4, 13. 14; the brothers of Joseph, Gen. 42, 21; David after his great sin, Ps. 51; Herod, Matt. 14, 2; Judas, Matt. 27, 3-5; Felix, Acts 24, 25.

3. *Against whom may we sin?*

Against God, against our neighbor, and against ourselves.

4. *How is sin divided?*

Into original or inborn sin, and actual sin.

5. *What is inborn, or hereditary sin?*

The natural depravity or sinful disposition which we inherit from our first parents.

* Ps. 51, 5. Behold, I was shapen in iniquity; and in sin did my mother conceive me.
* John 3, 6. That which is born of the flesh is flesh; and that which is born of the Spirit is spirit.
Job 14, 4. Who can bring a clean thing out of an unclean? not one.
Rom. 5, 12 (By one man sin entered into the world); Eph. 2, 3 ("We were by nature the children of wrath",—which teaches, also, original *guilt*); Luke 11, 13 (If ye, then, being evil).

6. *Wherein does this natural depravity consist?*

In this, that man, without the aid of divine grace, is opposed to good and prone to all evil.

7. *What is actual sin?*

All evil thoughts, words, and deeds.

* Matt. 15, 19. Out of the heart proceed evil thoughts, murders, adulteries, fornications, thefts, false witness, blasphemies.
Gal. 5, 19–21. The works of the flesh are manifest, which are these: Adultery, fornication, uncleanness, lasciviousness, idolatry, witchcraft, hatred, variance, emulations, wrath, strife, seditions, heresies, envyings, murders, drunkenness, revellings, and such like; of the which I tell you before, as I told you in time past, that they which do such things shall not inherit the kingdom of God.
Matt. 12, 36. Every idle *word* that men shall speak, they shall give account thereof in the day of judgment.

8. *How do you distinguish actual sins?*

Into sins of commission, and sins of omission.

9. *What is a sin of commission?*

The doing of what God has forbidden.

10. *What is a sin of omission?*

The leaving undone what God has commanded us to do.

* James 4, 17. To him that knoweth to do good, and doeth it not, to him it is sin.
Luke 12, 47. 48. That servant which knew his Lord's will, and prepared not himself, neither did according to his will, shall be beaten with many stripes. But he that knew not, and did commit things worthy of stripes, shall be beaten with few stripes.

11. *How again are actual sins divided?*

Into sins of weakness, and sins of malice.

12. *What is a sin of weakness?*

A sin of ignorance or carelessness, followed by sincere repentance, as in the case of David and Peter.

* Gal. 6, 1. Brethren, if a man be overtaken in a fault, ye which are spiritual, restore such an one in the spirit of meekness: considering thyself, lest thou also be tempted.
1 John 5, 16 ("a sin which is not unto death," as distinct from "a sin unto death").—Comp. David's fall and repentance, Ps. 51, and Peter's denial and repentance, Matt. 26, 69 ff; John 18, 17 ff; 21, 15 ff.

13. *What is a sin of malice?*

A sin which is committed knowingly and wilfully.

14. *Can all sins be forgiven?*

All sins can be forgiven for Christ's sake on condition of repentance, with the only exception of the blasphemy against the Holy Ghost, or total and final impenitence.

Heb. 10, 26. 27. If we sin wilfully after that we have received the knowledge of the truth, there remaineth no more sacrifice for sins, but a certain fearful looking for of judgment and fiery indignation, which shall devour the adversaries.
Heb. 6, 4–7 (of total apostasy); 1 John 5, 16 (of the sin unto death); 2 Pet. 2, 20–22.

Matt. 12, 31. All manner of sin and blasphemy shall be forgiven unto men; but the blasphemy against the Holy Ghost shall not be forgiven unto men.

NOTES AND HINTS.

Q. 2. *Conscience,* is the moral sense within us, or the natural, unwritten law common to all men, even the heathen (Rom. 2, 14. 15). The revealed and written law is summarily contained in the Ten Commandments, and these again resolve themselves into the two commandments of love to God, and love to our neighbor.—Comp. Lesson XLI.

Q. 3. (1.) Sins against *God:* all the violations of the first table, or the first four commandments, as idolatry, image-worship, perjury, cursing, swearing, blasphemy, irreverence, desecration of the sabbath, also disobedience, ingratitude, infidelity, mockery, and despair. (2.) Sins against our *neighbor:* all the violations of the second table, as murder, adultery, theft, slander, envy, jealousy, hatred, wrath. (3.) Sins against *ourselves:* avarice, intemperance, uncleanness, and all kinds of abuse of the faculties of body or soul. But all sins are both sins against God and against ourselves, because they are all transgressions of his holy law, and tend to our ruin.

Q. 6. Natural depravity may also be defined, more accurately, to consist in *the disorder of our moral nature and the perverse tendency of the will towards all that is evil.*

Q. 14. Hence the distinction between *pardonable* and *unpardonable* sins. But wherever there is sincere grief for, and repentance of, sin, it is sufficient evidence that the terrible sin against the Holy Ghost has not been committed. There is no certain example in the Bible of such a sin, unless it be the treason of Judas.

XXI. Punishment of Sin.

1. *What have we deserved by our sins?*

God's righteous wrath and punishment.

* Rom. 1, 18. The wrath [*i.e.* the punitive justice] of God is revealed from heaven against all ungodliness and unrighteousness of men, who hold [or rather, hold back, hinder] the truth in unrighteousness.

John 3, 36. He that believeth not the Son shall not see life; but the wrath of God abideth on him.

Gal. 3, 10. Cursed is every one that continueth not in all things which are written in the book of the law to do them.—Comp. Deut. 27, 26; Jer. 11, 3.

EXAMPLES of punishment: The fallen angels, Jude 6; 2 Pet. 2, 4; Adam and Eve and their expulsion from paradise, Gen. 3, 14–24; the generation of the flood, Gen. 6–8; Sodom and Gomorrha, Gen. 19, 24; 2 Pet. 2, 6; Lot's wife, Gen. 19, 26; Pharaoh and the Egyptians, Ex. 14, 23–28, etc., etc.

2. *Why does God punish sin?*

Because God is holy and just.

* Ps. 5, 4. Thou art not a God that hath pleasure in wickedness: neither shall evil dwell with thee.

* Hab. 1, 13. Thou art of purer eyes than to behold evil, and canst not look on iniquity.

3. How does God punish sin?

With temporal and eternal death.

* Ezek. 18, 4. The soul that sinneth, it shall die.

Rom. 5, 12. By one man sin entered into the world, and death by sin, and so death passed upon all men, for that all have sinned.

Rom. 6, 23. The wages of sin is death.

James 1, 15. When lust hath conceived, it bringeth forth sin; and sin, when it is finished, bringeth forth death.

Gen. 2, 17. In the day that thou eatest thereof, thou shalt surely die.

Gen. 3, 14–19; Heb. 10, 31; 12, 29; Gal. 6, 7. 8.

4. What are the temporal punishments of sin?

A bad conscience, sickness, all sorts of evil and misery, and physical death.

* Isa. 48, 22. There is no peace unto the wicked.—Comp. 57, 21.

Rom. 2, 8. 9. Indignation and wrath, tribulation and anguish, upon every soul of man that doeth evil.

* Rom. 6, 23. The wages of sin is death.

Comp. Gen. 2, 17; 3, 14–19; Rom. 5, 12.

5. But have not the children of God also to suffer affliction and death?

Yes; but God causes the sufferings of this life to advance the believer in holiness, and to prepare him for the joys of heaven.

* Prov. 3, 12. Whom the Lord loveth, he correcteth; even as a father the son in whom he delighteth.—Comp. Heb. 12, 6; Ps. 94, 12.

Rom. 5, 3–5. We glory in tribulations also: knowing that tribulation worketh patience; and patience, experience; and experience, hope; and hope maketh not ashamed; because the love of God is shed abroad in our hearts by the Holy Ghost which is given unto us.

Rom. 8, 18. I reckon that the sufferings of this present

time are not worthy to be compared with the glory that shall be revealed in us.

* 2 Cor. 4, 17. Our light affliction, which is but for a moment, worketh for us a far more exceeding and eternal weight of glory.

James 1, 12. Blessed is the man that endureth temptation: for when he is tried, he shall receive the crown of life, which the Lord hath promised to them that love him.

Job 5, 17; Ps. 94, 12; Matt. 5, 11. 12; Heb. 12, 6; 1 Pet. 1, 6. 7; 4, 12. 13; Rev. 3, 12. 19.

6. *Wherein does the eternal punishment of sin consist?*

In the entire separation of the sinner from God, and the endless pains of hell.

* Matt. 25, 41. Then shall he say also unto them on the left hand: Depart from me, ye cursed, into everlasting fire, prepared for the devil and his angels.

Comp. Matt. 25, 30 (outer darkness, weeping and gnashing of teeth); v. 46 (everlasting punishment); Dan. 12, 2 (some shall awake to shame and everlasting contempt); John 5, 29 (the resurrection of damnation); Mark 9, 44 (where their worm dieth not, and the fire is not quenched,—comp. Isa. 66, 24); Rev. 14, 10. 11 (the smoke of their torment ascendeth up for ever and ever); 20, 10.

7. *Will God punish all sinners alike?*

God punishes every sinner according to the degree of his guilt.

Luke 12, 47. 48. That servant which knew his lord's will, and prepared not himself, neither did according to his will, shall be beaten with many stripes. But he that knew not, and did commit things worthy of stripes, shall be beaten with few stripes. For unto whomsoever much is given, of him shall be much required.

Matt. 11, 21–24. Woe unto thee, Chorazin! woe unto thee, Bethsaida! . . . It shall be more tolerable for Tyre and Sidon at the day of judgment, than for you. And thou, Capernaum, which art exalted unto heaven, shalt be brought down to hell. . . . It shall be more tolerable for the land of Sodom in the day of judgment, than for thee.

Rom. 2, 12. As many as have sinned without law shall

also perish without law; and as many as have sinned in the law shall be judged by the law.
Comp. Matt. 10, 15; 5, 21. 22; John 9, 41; 15, 22. 24.

8. *Can we deliver ourselves from sin?*

By no means; but, if left to ourselves, we daily increase our guilt.

Ps. 49, 7. None of them can by any means redeem his brother, nor give to God a ransom for him.
Job 9, 2. 3. How should man be just with God? If he will contend with him, he cannot answer him one of a thousand.
* Rom. 7, 24. O wretched man that I am! who shall deliver me from the body of this death?

NOTES AND HINTS.

Q. 3. In these and many other passages *death* is a comprehensive term for all temporal and eternal evil. Hence, eternal damnation is sometimes called the *second* death, Rev. 2, 11; 20, 6. 14; 21, 8.

Q. 7. The passages there quoted fully justify the theory of various degrees of punishment, corresponding to various degrees of wickedness and guilt; so, on the other hand, there are also different degrees of beatitude in heaven, corresponding to different degrees of holiness.— Compare the parable of the talents, Matt. 25, 15–30, and the parable of the pounds, Luke 19, 12–26. The Jews will be more severely judged than the ignorant heathen; Christians, more severely than the Jews; and among Christians, again, the degree of condemnation will differ according to age, talent, knowledge, and opportunity.

XXII. Preparation for Salvation.

1. *Did God leave man to the power of sin and death?*

No: God has wrought out an everlasting salvation.

* Isa. 45, 17. Israel shall be saved in the Lord with an everlasting salvation.
Heb. 9, 12. ... having obtained eternal redemption for us.

2. *What do you mean by salvation?*

Deliverance from sin and death, and the reunion of man with God through Jesus Christ.

3. *Why has God wrought out such salvation?*

Because God is love, and has no pleasure in the death of the sinner.

* 1 Tim. 2, 4. God will have all men to be saved, and to come to the knowledge of the truth.
Ezek. 33, 11. As I live, saith the Lord God, I have no pleasure in the death of the wicked; but that the wicked turn from his way and live: turn ye, turn ye, from your evil ways; for why will ye die, O house of Israel?
2 Pet. 3, 9. The Lord is longsuffering to us-ward, not willing that any should perish, but that all should come to repentance.
* John 3, 16. God so loved the world that he gave his only begotten Son, that whosoever believeth in him should not perish, but have everlasting life.

4. *Will all men, then, be saved?*

Only those will be saved who believe in Jesus Christ and accept his benefits.

* Matt. 7, 13. 14. Enter ye in at the strait gate: for wide is the gate, and broad is the way, that leadeth to destruction, and many there be which go in thereat: because strait is the gate, and narrow is the way, which leadeth unto life, and few there be that find it.
John 3, 36. He that believeth on the Son hath everlasting life: and he that believeth not the Son shall not see life; but the wrath of God abideth on him.
Mark 16, 16. He that believeth and is baptized shall be saved; but he that believeth not shall be damned.

5. *When did God determine to save men?*

From eternity.

* Eph. 1, 4. According as he hath chosen us in him before the foundation of the world, that we should be holy and without blame before him in love.
Matt. 25, 34 (the kingdom prepared for you from the foundation of the world); Eph. 1, 11 (predestinated); 2 Tim. 1, 9 (before the world began); 1 Pet. 1, 20 (foreordained before the foundation of the world); Rev. 13, 8 (the Lamb slain from the foundation of the world); 17, 8 (written in the book of life from the foundation of the world).

PREPARATION FOR SALVATION.

6. *When did he first promise salvation?*

Immediately after the fall, when he said that the seed of the woman should bruise the serpent's head.

Gen. 3, 15. I will put enmity between thee [the devil in the disguise of the serpent] and the woman, and between thy seed and her seed: it shall bruise thy head, and thou shalt bruise his heel. [An allusion to the crucifixion, by which the tyranny of Satan was broken.]

7. *What does this mean?*

Christ will destroy the power of sin and of the devil.

* 1 John 3, 8. For this purpose the Son of God was manifested, that he might destroy the works of the devil.

8. *Through whom did God further promise salvation?*

Through the patriarchs Abraham, Isaac, and Jacob, through Moses, and the prophets of the old dispensation.

* Acts 10, 43. To him [Christ] give all the prophets witness.

Heb. 1, 1. 2. God, who at sundry times and in divers manners spake in times past unto the fathers by the prophets, hath in these last days spoken unto us by his Son.

Comp. Gen. 12, 1–3; 18, 8; 22, 8; 26, 4; 28, 14; 49, 8–10 (promises to the patriarchs); Deut. 18, 15–19 (prophecy of Moses); Rom. 1, 1. 2.

9. *Did God also foreshadow salvation?*

Yes: in the law, in the worship, and the whole history, of the people of Israel.

Heb. 10, 1 (the law having a shadow of good things to come, and not the very image of the things); Rom. 15, 4; 1 Cor. 10, 6.

10. *Who was the last prophet of the old dispensation?*

John the Baptist.

11. *What was the mission of John the Baptist?*

He prepared the way of the Lord, and

pointed to the Lamb of God which taketh away the sin of the world.

Isa. 40, 3–5; Mal. 3, 1; 4, 5; Matt. 3, 1–12; Mark 1, 2–8; Luke 3, 2–20; John 1, 29; Matt. 11, 7–14.

12. *When did God carry out the plan of salvation?*

When the time of preparation was fulfilled.

Mark 1, 15. The time is fulfilled.

* Gal. 4, 4. When the fulness of the time was come, God sent forth his Son.

13. *Through whom did God carry out the plan of salvation?*

Through his only begotten Son, Jesus Christ.

* 1 Tim. 1, 15. This is a faithful saying, and worthy of all acceptation, that Christ Jesus came into the world to save sinners.

NOTES AND HINTS.

Q. 8. *Special* prophecies concerning Christ: His *descent* from Abraham, Gen. 12, 3; 18, 18; 22, 18; from the tribe of Judah, Gen. 49, 10; from the house of David, 2 Sam. 7, 16; Isa. 11, 1; from a Virgin, Isa. 7, 14; Matt. 1, 23; the *place* of his birth, Mic. 5, 2; the *time* of his birth, Dan. 9, 24. 25; his *forerunner*, Mal. 3, 1; Isa. 40, 3–5; his *poverty* and *lowliness*, Zech. 9, 9; Isa. 53, 3; his *sufferings* and *death*, Gen. 3, 15; Ps. 22, 1–20 (comp. Matt. 27, 46; John 19, 23. 24); Zech. 11, 11–14; Isa. 53, 4–7; his *resurrection* and *exaltation*, Ps. 2, 6. 7 (comp. Acts 13, 13; Heb. 1, 5; 5, 3); Ps. 16, 10 (comp. Acts 2, 30. 31; 13, 35–37); Isa. 53, 9–12; his *prophetic* office, Deut. 18, 18. 19; his atoning *sacrifice*, Isa. 53, 4–6; his eternal *priesthood*, Ps. 110, 4 (comp. Heb. 5, 6; 6, 20; 7, 17. 21); his eternal *kingdom*, Ps. 2, 6. 7; 110, 1–4; Zech. 9, 10; Dan. 7, 13. 14.

Q. 9. The Old Testament is full of *types* which prefigure and foreshadow the person and work of Christ. We may distinguish typical institutions, facts, and persons.

(1.) Typical INSTITUTIONS: *Circumcision* (Rom. 4, 11; Col. 2, 11. 12); the *sacrifices* (Lev. 17, 11; Heb. 9, 22–25; 10, 1–4), especially the *paschal lamb* (Ex. 12; John 1, 29; 1 Cor. 5, 7), and generally the whole ritual or ceremonial *law*, and Mosaic *worship*.

(2.) Typical EVENTS: The sacrifice of Isaac (Heb. 11, 19); the elevation of the brazen serpent in the wilderness (Num. 21, 4–9; John 3, 14); the redemption of Israel from the bondage of Egypt, and subsequently from the captivity of Babylon.

(3.) Typical PERSONS: *Adam* as the patriarch of the human family, or the representative man (Rom. 5, 14); *Melchizedek* as a priest-king (Gen. 14, 17–20; Ps. 110, 4; Heb. 7); *Moses* as the deliverer and lawgiver of Israel (Deut. 18, 18. 19); *Joshua* as the leader of Israel on their passage into Canaan (Heb. 4, 8–10); *David* as a victorious king (Ps. 2 and 110); *Solomon* as a king of peace (2 Sam. 7, 12–15), and generally all the prophets, priests, and kings of Israel in their *official* (not in their *personal*) character.

Q. 11. John the Baptist is the *personal representative of the whole Old Testament* in its direct tendency toward the New dispensation. He combines in his person the rigor of the *law* in his ascetic mode of life and earnest call to repentance, and the comfort of the *promise* in his pointing to the Lamb o" God which taketh away the sin of the world. He immediately preceded Christ, as the dawn of morning precedes the rising of the sun, and delighted to decrease, in order that Christ might increase. He is in his official character the greatest of those that were born of women before Christ, because he stood nearest to Christ; yet smaller than the least in the kingdom of heaven, because he still belonged to the preparatory dispensation of Judaism, and stood, during his earthly life, merely in the outer court of the Christian salvation. Comp. Matt. 11, 11.

XXIII. Jesus Christ.—His Names.

1. *What do you believe concerning Jesus Christ?*

I believe in Jesus Christ, God's only begotten Son our Lord; who was conceived by the Holy Ghost, born of the Virgin Mary; suffered under Pontius Pilate, was crucified, dead, and buried; He descended into hades; the third day He rose from the dead; He ascended into heaven; and sitteth at the right hand of God the Father Almighty; from thence He shall come to judge the quick and the dead.

2. *What does the name Jesus signify?*

Jesus means a Saviour.

3. *Why is he so called?*

Because he saves us from sin and death.

Ps. 130, 8. He shall redeem Israel from all his iniquities.

* Matt. 1, 21. She [Mary] shall bring forth a son, and thou shalt call his name JESUS: for he shall save his people from their sins.

Luke 1, 31; 19, 10; Acts 5, 31; 1 Tim. 1, 15.

4. *What does the name Christ signify?*

Christ, or Messiah, means the Anointed.

John 1, 41. We have found the Messias, which is, being interpreted, the Christ [or, the Anointed].

5. *Why is he so called?*

Because he was anointed with the Holy Spirit to be our perfect and eternal Prophet, Priest, and King.

Isa. 61, 1. The Spirit of the Lord God is upon me; because the Lord hath anointed me to preach good tidings unto the meek.—Comp. Luke 4, 18.

Luke 3, 22. And the Holy Ghost descended [at the baptism of Jesus] in a bodily shape like a dove upon him.

Acts 10, 38. How God anointed Jesus of Nazareth with the Holy Ghost and with power.

6. *Why are believers called Christians?*

Because, being united to Christ by faith, and partakers of his anointing, they should follow his example and be transformed more and more into his holy image.

Acts 11, 26. The disciples [of Jesus] were called Christians first at Antioch.

Eph. 5, 30. We are members of his body, of his flesh, and of his bones.

1 John 2, 20. Ye have an unction from the Holy One, and ye know all things.

1 John 2, 27. The anointing which ye have received of him, abideth in you.

* 1 Pet. 2, 9. Ye are a chosen generation, a royal priesthood, a holy nation, a peculiar people; that ye should show forth the praises of him who hath called you out of darkness into his marvellous light.

1 John 3, 2. Beloved, now are we the sons of God, and it doeth not yet appear what we shall be: but we know that, when he shall appear, we shall be like him; for we shall see him as he is. 1 Pet. 2, 21; Rom. 8, 29; Rev. 2, 5.

NOTE.

Q. 2–4. *Jesus* and *Messiah* are from the Hebrew, *Christ* from the Greek. *Jesus* is the same with *Joshua*, i. e. Jehovah's salvation, Jehovah is Saviour. This is the *personal* name of our Lord given to him by divine command at his circumcision, and its meaning was fulfilled in him, and in him alone. It is the sweetest name, a balm to the sinner, a delight to the believer, a terror to the devil. *Christ* is his *official* name, and is applied to him exclusively. Hence, John 20, 31, "These [signs] are written that ye might believe that *Jesus is the* [promised and long-expected] *Christ*, the Son of God."

XXIV. Of the Person of Christ.

1. *What do you believe concerning the person of Christ?*

Jesus Christ is the God-man, or true God and true man in one person forever.

2. *Why must he unite the divine and human natures in his person?*

That he might be the mediator between God and man, and reconcile them.

* 1 Tim. 2, 5. 6. There is one God, and one mediator between God and men, the man Christ Jesus, who gave himself a ransom for all.

2 Cor. 5, 19. God was in Christ, reconciling the world to himself.

3. *How do you prove the true divinity of Christ?*

From the divine names, the divine attributes, the divine works, and the divine honors, of Christ.

* John 10, 30. I and my Father are one.

John 1, 1. In the beginning [*i.e.* from eternity] was the Word [Christ as to his divine nature, comp. v. 14], and the Word was with God, and the Word was God [of divine essence].

* Col. 2, 9. In Christ dwelleth all the fulness of the Godhead bodily.

Col. 1, 15. 16. Who is the image of the invisible God, the first-born of every creature; for by him were all things created that are in heaven and that are in earth, visible and invisible.

Heb. 1, 3. Who being the brightness of his [God's] glory, and the express image of his person, and upholding all things by the word of his power.

Heb. 1, 16. Let all the angels of God worship him.

* John 20, 28. Thomas answered and said unto him: My Lord and my God.

1 John 5, 20. This [*i.e.* his Son Jesus Christ] is the true God and eternal life.

Rev. 17, 14. He is Lord of lords, and King of kings.

OF THE PERSON OF CHRIST.

4. *How do you prove the true humanity of Christ?*

From his birth, his growth, his temptation, his sufferings, his death and burial.

* John 1, 14. And the Word [*i.e.* the eternal, only begotten Son of God, or Christ according to his divine nature, comp. v. 1] was made flesh [assumed human nature, or became man], and dwelt among us.

Heb. 2, 14. As the children [of man] are partakers of flesh and blood, he also himself likewise took part of the same.

Rom. 1, 3. Concerning his Son Jesus Christ our Lord, which was made of the seed of David according to the flesh [*i.e.* his visible earthly human nature].

Phil. 2, 7. He made himself of no reputation, and took upon him the form of a servant, and was made in the likeness of men.

1 Tim. 3, 16. God was manifest in the flesh.

Comp. Rom. 5, 15 (by one man, Jesus Christ); 8, 3 (in the likeness of sinful flesh); 1 Tim. 2, 5 (the man Christ Jesus); 1 John 4, 2 (Jesus Christ is come in the flesh).

5. *Did Christ become like us in all things?*

Yes: in all things, sin only excepted.

* Heb. 4, 15. He was in all points tempted like as we are, yet without sin.

6. *What do you mean by the sinlessness of Jesus?*

His freedom from original and actual sin, and his perfect holiness.

* John 8, 46. Which of you convinceth me of sin?

* 2 Cor. 5, 21. He hath made him to be sin for us, who knew no sin; that we might be made the righteousness of God in him.

1 Pet. 2, 22. Who did no sin, neither was guile found in his mouth.—Comp. Isa. 53, 9.

1 John 3, 5. He was manifested to take away our sins; and in him is no sin.

Heb. 7, 26. Such a high priest became us, who is holy, harmless, undefiled, separate from sinners, and made higher than the heavens.

7. *Was Christ not tempted like the first Adam?*

Yes: he was tempted by the devil, but he

overcame temptation, fulfilled the law, and revealed righteousness and life.

Matt. 4, 1–10 (comp. Mark 1, 12. 13; Luke 4, 1–12).

* Heb. 4, 15. We have not a high priest which cannot be touched with the feeling of our infirmities; but was in all points tempted like as we are, yet without sin.—Comp. 5, 7–9; Luke 22, 28.

Rom. 5, 18. As by the offence of one [Adam], judgment came upon all men to condemnation; even so by the righteousness of one [Christ], the free gift came upon all men unto justification of life.

NOTES AND HINTS.

Q. 3. The principal arguments for the divinity of Christ are—

(1.) The divine NAMES of Christ. He is called "*the Son of God*" (not a Son simply among others, but *the* Son in the highest or absolute sense, as he is called "*the* Son of man"), John 6, 69; Matt. 26, 63. 64, and often; "*the only begotten Son of God,*" John 1, 14; 3, 16; 1 John 4, 9; "*Emmanuel,*" i.e. *God with us*, Matt. 1, 23 (Isa. 7, 14); "*Lord,*" Ps. 110, 1; Acts 1, 21, and often; "*Lord and God,*" John 20, 28; "*God,*" John 1, 1; "*the great God and Saviour,*" Tit. 2, 13; "*the true God and eternal life,*" 1 John 5, 20; "*God blessed forever,*" Rom. 9, 5 (which refers to the preceding "Christ.")

(2.) Divine ATTRIBUTES of Christ: *eternity*, John 1, 1 ("in the beginning," i.e. before the world, comp. v. 3, or, from everlasting); 8, 58 ("*Before* Abraham *was*, I *am*"); 17, 5 ("the glory which I had with thee *before the world was*"); Col. 1, 15–17; Rev. 1, 8 ("I am *Alpha* and Omega, the *beginning* and the ending"). *Omnipotence*, John 3, 35 ("the Father loveth the Son, and hath *given all things into his hand*"); 10, 30; Matt. 11, 27; 28, 18 ("*All power* is given unto me in heaven and in earth"); John 14, 14; Eph. 1, 21; Phil. 3, 21 ("he is able even to subdue all things unto himself"); Rev. 1, 8 ("the Almighty"). *Omnipresence*, Matt. 18, 20; 28, 20. *Omniscience*, John 1, 18; 6, 46; 10, 15; Matt. 11, 27; John 21, 17; Rev. 2, 23. *Unchangeableness*, Heb. 13, 8.—Comp. in general Col. 1, 19; 2, 9.

(3.) Divine WORKS: The *creation* of the world, John 1, 3; Col. 1, 16. 17; Heb. 1, 2. The *redemption*, Tit. 2, 4; 1 Cor. 6, 20; 1 Pet. 1, 18. 19. The last *judgment*, John 5, 22; Matt. 25, 31. 32; Rom. 14, 10; 2 Cor. 5, 10.

(4.) Divine HONORS: John 5, 23 ("that all men should honor the Son, even as they honor the Father"); Phil. 2, 10 ("that at the name of Jesus every knee should bow"); Heb. 1, 6 (comp. Ps. 97, 7;) Rev. 1, 6; 5, 12.

Q. 4. The *human* nature of Christ includes a true human *body, soul,* and *spirit*. All essential attributes and conditions of man are ascribed to him. He calls himself with condescending love and sympathy, about eighty times in the Gospels, *the Son of man* (while the apostles generally call him *the Son of God*), and this term implies both his equality with us (Son of man), and his surpassing excellency (*the* Son of man) as the perfect man in whom alone the idea of humanity has been fully realized. He assumed our *flesh* and *blood*, John 1, 14; Heb. 2, 14; he was *born* in Bethlehem of a woman, Luke 2, 7; Gal. 4, 4; he *grew, waxed* strong in spirit, and *increased* in wisdom and stature, Luke 2, 40. 52; he passed through the different *ages* of human existence from infancy to boyhood youth, and manhood (with the exception of declining old age, which seems incompatible with the idea of the Saviour, who died and rose and lives forever in the unbroken vigor and freshness of early manhood); he was *tempted*, Matt. 4, 1; Heb. 2, 18; 4, 15; he *learned* obedience, Heb. 5, 8; he *hungered*, Matt. 4, 2, and *thirsted*, John 4, 7; 19, 28; he was *wearied*, John 4, 6; he did *eat* and *drink*, Matt. 11, 19; he *slept*, Matt. 8, 14; he *wept* tears of sorrow over unbelieving Jerusalem, Luke 19, 41, tears of friendship at the grave of Lazarus, John 11, 35, and tears of sympathetic anguish in Gethsemane, Luke 22, 44; comp. Heb. 5, 7 (but it is never said that he *laughed*, because this would hardly comport with his dignity and solemn mission); he was *troubled* in his *soul*, John 12, 27, and exceeding *sorrowful*, Matt. 26, 38; he *shed blood* on the cross, John 19, 33. 34; he *suffered* and *died*, 19, 30–34, and was *buried*, 19, 40–42; he had *flesh* and *blood* even *after* his resurrection, Luke 24, 39; he retained his *wounds*, John 20, 27; he ascended *visibly* to heaven, Acts 1, 9, and shall *visibly* return, though not in the form of a servant, but in glory, 1, 11; Matt. 25, 31.

Q. 6. The perfect *sinlessness* of Jesus may be proved:

(1.) By *his own* history and testimony. For he never said or did any thing which he had reason to regret; he never felt himself a sinner or asked the forgiveness of God (the petition in the Lord's Prayer: "Forgive us our debts," is intended for his followers only); he was in no need of conversion and regeneration, or even reform and improvement, as all other men are, and in the triumphant consciousness of his spotless purity he could boldly challenge his bitter enemies to convict him of sin, without fear of the result, John 8, 46.

(2.) By the testimony of his *friends*, the apostles and evangelists, who from personal observation exempt him from all moral defects and pronounce him pure and holy.—(Comp., besides the passages quoted above, Acts 3, 14; 1 Pet. 1, 19; 3, 18; 1 John 2, 29; 3, 7; Heb. 4, 15.)

(3.) By the testimony of his *enemies*,—Pontius Pilate, who, although his human judge, representing the majesty of the Roman law, evidently trembled before Christ, and washed his hands to be clean of innocent blood (Matt. 27, 24; Luke 23, 22); the rude heathen centurion, who exclaimed under the cross: "Truly this was a righteous man, and the Son of God" (Matt. 27, 54; Luke 23, 47); and Judas the traitor, who confessed, in despair: "I have betrayed innocent blood," (Matt. 27, 4).

The sinlessness of Christ, viewed under its positive aspect, is absolute holiness, or moral perfection, the ideal of human virtue fully actualized, perfect love to God and to man, combining all active and passive virtues and the opposite graces in full harmony and symmetry.

The sinlessness of the Saviour, contrasted with the sinful world, is the one absolute exception to the universal rule, a miracle in history, raising him far above all other men, and can only be fully accounted for by the indwelling of the fulness of the Godhead in him.

XXV. The Two States of Christ.

1. *What are the two states or conditions in the history of Christ?*

The state of humiliation, and the state of exaltation.

Phil. 2, 5-11.—Comp. 2 Cor. 8, 9; Eph. 4, 9. 10; Heb. 2, 9-11.

2. *What do you mean by the humiliation of Christ?*

From infinite love to us, he freely laid aside his divine glory and majesty, and took upon himself the form of a servant.

3. *What belongs to the state of humiliation?*

Christ's conception and birth, his passion and death, his burial, and descent into hades.

4. *What do you mean by the exaltation of Christ?*

After completing the work of redemption, he returned to the full possession of his eternal divine glory, and raised human nature to a share in this glory.

John 17, 5. O Father, glorify thou me with thine own self, with the glory which I had with thee before the world was.

John 17, 24. Father, I will that they also, whom thou hast given me, be with me where I am; that they may behold my glory, which thou hast given me.

5. *What are the stages of his exaltation?*

His resurrection, his ascension, his sitting at the right hand of God, and his return to judgment.

6. *What do you learn from the two states of Christ?*

That I should follow my Saviour in the path of humility and self-denial, so that I may become partaker also of his divine glory and majesty.

* Phil. 2, 5–7. Let this mind be in you, which was also in Christ Jesus: who, being in the form of God, thought it no robbery to be equal with God, but made himself of no reputation, and took upon himself the form of a servant.
2 Tim. 2, 11. 12. If we be dead with Christ, we shall also live with him; if we suffer, we shall also reign with him.
' Matt. 5, 11. 12; Rom. 8, 17; 2 Cor. 4, 10; 1 Pet. 4, 13; Rev. 3, 21.

XXVI. Birth and Childhood of Jesus.

1. *What do you believe concerning the birth of Jesus?*

He was conceived by the Holy Spirit, and born of the Virgin Mary, of the house of David, a true man, yet without sin.

* Luke 1, 35. And the angel [Gabriel] answered and said unto her [Mary]: The Holy Ghost shall come upon thee, and the power of the Highest shall overshadow thee: therefore also that holy thing which shall be born of thee, shall be called the Son of God.
Matt. 1, 18; John 1, 14; Gal. 4, 4; Heb. 2, 14. 15; 1 Tim. 3, 16.

2. *Why did the eternal Son of God take our human nature into fellowship with his divine person?*

In order that he might live, suffer, die, and rise again for us, and thus accomplish in our nature the redemption of man.

* Gal. 4, 4. 5. When the fulness of the time was come, God sent forth his Son, made of a woman, made under the law, to redeem them that were under the law, that we might receive the adoption of sons.
Matt. 20, 28; Tit. 2, 14; Heb. 9, 12.

3. *When was Jesus born?*

During the reign of Augustus, the Roman

emperor, and Herod the Great, the king of the Jews.

Luke 2, 1; Matt. 2, 1.

4. *Where was Jesus born?*
At Bethlehem in Judea.

Micah 5, 2; Matt. 2, 1; Luke 2, 4. 7. 12.

5. *Why was Jesus born in such a lowly condition?*
That by his poverty he might make us rich, and draw even the humblest to himself.

* 2 Cor. 8, 9. Ye know the grace of our Lord Jesus Christ, that, though he was rich, yet for your sakes he became poor, that ye through his poverty might be rich.—Comp. Luke 9, 58.

6. *What did the angels in heaven do at the birth of Jesus?*
They rejoiced, and sang: "Glory to God in the highest, and on earth peace, good will toward men."

Luke 2, 14.

7. *What else took place at the birth of Jesus?*
The Jewish shepherds came from the field, and the heathen sages from the East, and worshipped the child.

Luke 2, 15–20; Matt. 2, 1–11.

8. *What occurred on the eighth day after Christ's birth?*
He was circumcised according to the custom of the Jews, and called JESUS.

Luke 2, 21; Matt. 1, 21. (Gen. 17, 22.)

9. *What do you know of the childhood of Jesus?*
When he was twelve years old, he sat in

the temple of Jerusalem, in the midst of the doctors, both hearing them and asking them questions, and had his chief delight in religion.
Luke 2, 46–49.

10. *What else is reported of Jesus in his youth?*
That he was subject to his parents, an increased in wisdom, and stature, and in favor with God and men.
Luke 2, 51. 52; Heb. 5, 8.

11. *What benefit do you derive from the birth and childhood of Jesus?*
He has redeemed our infancy and childhood, and consecrated them to God, and has left to children a perfect pattern of obedience.

NOTES AND HINTS.

Q. 5. The poverty and humility of Christ continued from his birth through his whole life on earth, since he had not where to lay his head (Luke 9, 58; Matt. 8, 21), and was supported by the benevolence of a few pious females (Luke 8, 3); the scanty purse being in the hands of a thief (John 12, 6). It was a part of his merciful condescension and humiliation for our elevation. But the poverty of his birth was, nevertheless, accompanied by glorious circumstances, the praises of angels in heaven, the adoration of the shepherds of Israel, and of the wise men from the distant East. The glory of the only begotten of the Father shone already from the infant in the manger, foreshadowing the mystery of the union of the divine and human, which was to unfold itself more and more in his life and work.

Q. 6. This is the so-called *Gloria in excelsis*, which ever since, in its original and amplified forms, resounds throughout Christendom in every tongue.

XXVII. Public Life and Work of Christ.

1. *Where and how did Jesus grow up?*
At Nazareth in Galilee, in poverty and humility, as the son of a carpenter.

Matt. 2, 23. And he came and dwelt in a city called Nazareth.
Matt. 13, 55. Is not this the carpenter's son? Is not his mother called Mary?
Mark 6, 3; Luke 2, 39; John 1, 45. 46; 6, 42.

2. *What took place before he commenced his public ministry?*

He was baptized in Jordan, by John the Baptist.

Matt. 3, 13–17; Luke 3, 21. 22; John 1, 32. 33.

3. *Why was he baptized?*

That he might fulfil all righteousness, and be solemnly consecrated to his public ministry.

Matt. 3, 15.

4. *What happened at the baptism of Jesus?*

The Holy Ghost descended upon him like a dove, and a voice from heaven said: "This is my beloved Son, in whom I am well pleased."

5. *What followed after the baptism of Jesus?*

He was tempted by the devil in the wilderness, as Adam and Eve were tempted in paradise, but he overcame the temptation.

Matt. 4, 1–11; Mark 1, 12 ff; Luke 4, 1 ff.—Comp. Lesson XXIV., Q. 7.

6. *When did Christ enter upon his public ministry?*

In the thirtieth year of his age.

Luke 3, 23. (Comp. Numb. 4, 3. 35. 39. 43. 47.)

7. *How long did his public life last?*

About three years.

8. *Wherein did it consist?*

He called and trained twelve apostles, taught

the purest doctrine, and confirmed it by the holiest life, and by many miracles of power and mercy.

Matt. 10, 1-4; Mark 3, 14-19.—Matt. 4, 23; Luke 8, 1; John 18, 20, and the whole evangelical history.

9. *What was the design of Christ?*

To found the kingdom of heaven on earth, which is to embrace the whole human family, and to last forever.

Matt. 8, 11; 16, 18. 19; 21, 43; 24, 14; 28, 19; John 4. 21-24; 10, 16; 18, 36. 37.

10. *By what means was Christ's kingdom to be founded and promoted?*

Not by force, nor any carnal weapons, but by spiritual and moral means, even his passion, death, and resurrection.

John 18, 36. My kingdom is not of this world: if my kingdom were of this world, then would my servants fight, that I should not be delivered to the Jews; but now is my kingdom not from hence.

2 Cor. 10, 4. The weapons of our warfare are not carnal, but mighty through God.

Acts 14, 22. We must through much tribulation enter into the kingdom of God.

John 6, 15; 12, 24. 25. 32; Matt. 10, 38; 16, 21-25; 26, 51-53; Luke 12, 14; 22, 28-30; 2 Tim. 2, 11. 12.

11. *Of what benefit is the public life of Christ to you?*

Christ is the perfect exemplar of piety and virtue, or of love to God and man, for our imitation.

John 12, 26. If any man serve me, let him follow me.

John 13, 15. I have given you an example, that ye should do as I have done to you.

John 15, 10; Matt. 20, 27. 28; Luke 9, 23; Phil. 2, 5; Col. 3, 13; 1 John 2, 6; 3, 16; 1 Pet. 2, 21.

Notes and Hints.

Q. 1. Joseph was, of course, only the *foster*-father of Jesus; but the Jews, who knew nothing of the mystery of the supernatural conception, regarded him as the *real* father. From Mark 6, 3, where Jesus is called "*the carpenter*" (not only "the carpenter's son," as in several other passages), it would appear that he actually took part in his father's trade, and thus dignified and ennobled even the humblest manual labor. Justin Martyr, in the beginning of the second century, says that Jesus performed the labors of a carpenter, and made ploughs and yokes. St. Paul also, in accordance with a Jewish custom, united a trade with his spiritual labors, being a tent-maker, Acts 18, 3.

Jesus attended the Jewish synagogue at Nazareth on sabbath-days (Luke 4, 16), and the temple of Jerusalem on high festivals (Luke 2, 42 ff). and was brought up under the influence of pious parents, the works of nature, and the Scriptures of the Old Testament; but he did not receive a learned education, and can not be classed either with school-trained nor with self-trained or self-made men. Hence the astonishment of the Jews: "How knoweth this man letters, having never learned?" (John 7, 15; comp. Mark 6, 2). His wisdom proceeded from no human or natural source, but directly from God, and surpassed all the learning and wisdom which human instruction and study can impart. He taught the world with authority, as one who was under no obligations to it, and who came out from God as the light of the world, and the truth itself in personal form.

Q. 5. The threefold temptation of Christ in the wilderness—the symbol of the moral ruin of the race after the fall—is the counterpart of the temptation of Adam in paradise,—the abode of original innocence and happiness. It was the Messianic *probation*, as the baptism in Jordan was the Messianic *inauguration*, and teaches us how to overcome all temptation to sin, by the word of God. The temptation, however, ran through the whole earthly life of Jesus, and culminated in the agony of Gethsemane and on the cross, where it was completely broken. —Comp. Luke 22, 28; Heb. 4, 15; 5, 7-9.

Q. 7. This view of the duration of his public ministry, which was prevalent in the early Church, is based upon the arrangement of John's Gospel according to three or four passovers during that ministry, and on Luke 13, 7, where the "three years" seem to contain an allusion to the time during which Christ addressed the unfruitful fig-tree, *i.e.* the Jewish nation.

Q. 9 and 10. The kingdom which Jesus came to found differs from all human schemes and institutions by its spiritual character, its universal extent, its eternal duration, and the spiritual mode of its establishment and promotion. The mere conception of such a design, which never entered the imagination of man before, forms a strong argument for his divine mission and character. Napoleon is reported to have said on St. Helena: "Alexander, Cæsar, Charlemagne, and myself founded empires on force, and they perished; Jesus of Nazareth alone, a crucified Jew, founded his kingdom on love; and at this hour millions of men would die for him." The history of the world before Christ prepared the way, and the history of the world since his coming, must subserve the spread and final triumph of this kingdom of truth and love and peace.

XXVIII. The Passion and Death of Jesus.

1. *When did Jesus suffer?*

During the whole period of his life on earth.

2. *What did he suffer?*

Poverty and sorrow, and the hatred and opposition of an ungodly world.

Isa. 53, 3. He is despised and rejected of men; a man of sorrows, and acquainted with grief.
Heb. 12, 3. Consider him that endured such contradiction of sinners against himself.
Luke 9, 58; John 15, 18. 20; Matt. 2, 13; 9, 36; 10, 25; 15, 16; Luke 12, 50; 19, 47, etc.

3. *When did he suffer most?*

At the end of his earthly life, in the garden of Gethsemane, before Caiaphas and Pontius Pilate, and on the cross.

The history of the Passion, Matt. 26 and 27; Mark 14 and 15; Luke 22 and 23; John 18 and 19.

4. *What did he suffer there?*

He suffered unutterable pains in body and soul, and bore the guilt of the whole world.

5. *Name the chief events of his passion.*

He was betrayed by Judas, taken prisoner, denied by Peter, dragged before the Jewish and heathen tribunals, mocked, scourged, crowned with thorns, unjustly condemned, and crucified between two malefactors.

6. *What death did Christ die?*

The most painful and ignominious death of the cross.

7. *How did he suffer all this?*

Like an innocent lamb, with the greatest meekness, patience, and resignation to the will of God.

* Isa. 53, 7. He was oppressed, and he was afflicted, yet he opened not his mouth: he is brought as a lamb to the slaughter, and as a sheep before her shearers is dumb, so he openeth not his mouth.—Comp. Matt. 26, 63; 27, 12. 14.

* Matt. 26, 39. O my Father, if it be possible, let this cup pass from me: nevertheless, not as I will, but as thou wilt.

1 Pet. 2, 23. Who, when he was reviled, reviled not again; when he suffered, he threatened not.

8. *Why did Christ thus suffer and die?*

Not for his sake, but in our stead, and for our benefit, out of free and boundless love.

* Isa. 53, 4. 5. Surely he hath borne our griefs, and carried our sorrows. ... He was wounded for our transgressions, he was bruised for our iniquities: the chastisement of our peace was upon him; and with his stripes we are healed.

Matt. 26, 28. This is my blood of the New Testament [or covenant], which is shed for many [as opposed, not to *all*, but to *few*] for the remission of sins.

* 2 Cor. 5, 21. God made him to be sin for us, who knew no sin; that we might be made the righteousness of God in him.

John 1, 29; 10, 12; 15, 13; Matt. 20, 28; Rom. 5, 8. 15; Heb. 9, 22.

9. *What benefit do you derive from Christ's passion and death?*

He has redeemed us from the guilt and power of sin, and reconciled us to God.

* John 1, 29. Behold the Lamb of God, which taketh away the sin of the world.

1 Cor. 15, 3. Christ died for our sins.

* 2 Cor. 5, 19. God was in Christ reconciling the world unto himself, not imputing their trespasses unto them.

Gal. 3, 13. Christ hath redeemed us from the curse of the law, being made a curse for us.

* 1 John 1, 7. The blood of Jesus Christ his Son cleanseth us from all sin.

1 John 2, 2; Rom. 5, 8–10; Col. 1, 20; 1 Pet. 2, 24; Heb. 2, 14. 15; Rev. 1, 5.

10. *What other benefit do you derive from it?*
He has left us an example of perfect gentleness, meekness, and patience under suffering.

* 1 Pet. 2, 21. Christ suffered for us, leaving us an example, that ye should follow his steps.
Heb. 12, 2; John 13, 15; Phil. 2, 5; 1 John 2, 6.

11. *What should you learn from Christ's passion?*
To be forever thankful to him, and to live no longer unto sin, but unto him only who died for us.

Gal. 2, 20. I am crucified with Christ: nevertheless I live; yet not I, but Christ liveth in me: and the life which I now live in the flesh I live by the faith of the Son of God, who loved me, and gave himself for me.
* 2 Cor. 5, 15. He died for all, that they which live should not henceforth live unto themselves, but unto him which died for them and rose again.
* Gal. 6, 14. God forbid that I should glory, save in the cross of our Lord Jesus Christ, by whom the world is crucified unto me, and I unto the world.
Rom. 6, 6; 14, 7–9; Gal. 5, 24; 1 Cor. 2, 2; 1 Pet. 4, 1. 2.

NOTES AND HINTS.

Q. 5. The *succession of events* in the history of the *Passion* from Thursday evening till Friday evening (probably on the 6th and 7th days of April):
1. The celebration of the Jewish passover. The emulation of the disciples, and the washing of feet. The institution of the Lord's Supper. Thursday evening.
2. The parting discourses and the intercessory prayer, John 14 to 17. Before midnight.
3. The crossing of Cedron, and the agony in the garden of Gethsemane. About midnight.
4. The kiss of Judas. The imprisonment. The flight of the disciples. Jesus before Annas. The denial of Peter. After midnight.
5. Jesus before Caiaphas and the Sanhedrim.
6. Jesus before Pontius Pilate, the Roman governor, and Herod, the king, then again before Pilate. About three o'clock on Friday morning.
7. The scourging, the crowning with thorns, and the condemnation to death. At six o'clock.
8. The carrying of the cross on the way to Golgotha outside of the city.
9. The crucifixion about nine o'clock [or the *third* hour, according to

the *Jewish* mode of counting from sunrise (six o'clock) to sunset, Mark 15, 25, with whom Matthew and Luke correspond. The *sixth* hour in John 19, 14, being the hour when the sentence of death was pronounced (No. 7), must be understood of the *Roman* mode of counting from midnight to midnight, *i.e.* six o'clock in the morning. Christ, therefore, hung on the cross six (not three) hours]. The two thieves. Mary and John. The seven words on the cross. The darkness from twelve to three o'clock P.M.

10. The death of Christ at three o'clock, P.M. The piercing of his side. The descent from the cross, and the burial, on Friday evening.

Q. 6. *Crucifixion* was one of the most painful and disgraceful modes of death. It was unusual among the Jews, and applied by the Romans (till Constantine the Great) only to slaves and gross criminals, as rebels and highway-robbers. Cicero calls it the most cruel and abominable punishment (*crudelissimum teterrimumque supplicium*). The cross consisted of two pieces of wood, generally put together in the form of a T. The longer beam was planted in the earth, and provided with a prominence in the middle for the body to rest upon. The victim was first undressed, the arms tied with ropes to the cross-beam, the hands fastened with iron nails, the feet tied or nailed to the upright post. In this unnatural and immovable position of the body, he suffered intensely from thirst, hunger, inflammation of the wounds, and deep anguish in consequence of the rushing of the blood towards the head. Death followed slowly from loss of blood, thirst and hunger, gradual exhaustion, and stiffening of the muscles, veins, and nerves. The sufferers lingered generally twelve hours,—sometimes, according to the strength of their constitution, to the second or third day. The bodies were left hanging on the cross until they decayed or were devoured by birds. But the Jews were accustomed to take them down and bury them.

XXIX. The Burial of Christ, and his Descent into Hades.

1. *What took place after the death of Jesus?*

His body was laid in a new sepulchre in a garden, by Joseph of Arimathea, and Nicodemus, but did not see corruption.

John 19, 38–42; Mark 15, 43–46; Luke 23, 52. 53: Matt 27, 66; Acts 13, 29; 1 Cor. 15, 4; Isa. 53, 9; Ps. 16, 10.—Comp. Acts 2, 31.

2. *What does the burial of Christ teach you?*

That he truly died, and completed the full measure of man's lot on earth.

3. *What comfort do you derive from the burial of Jesus?*

Christ has deprived the grave of its terrors, and consecrated it for believers, so that their bodies sleep in Jesus in the hope of a blessed resurrection.

* Phil. 1, 21. To me to live is Christ, and to die is gain.

* Rev. 14, 13. Blessed are the dead which die in the Lord from henceforth: Yea, saith the Spirit, that they may rest from their labors; and their works do follow them.

Comp. Rom. 6, 4; John 12, 24; 2 Tim. 1, 10; 1 Thess. 4, 14 (them which sleep in Jesus); Isa. 57, 2; Ps. 16, 10.

4. *Where was the soul of Christ while his body rested in the grave?*

In paradise, and in the region of departed spirits.

Luke 23, 43. And Jesus said unto him [the penitent thief]: Verily, I say unto thee, To-day thou shalt be with me in paradise. [Comp. "Abraham's bosom," Luke 16, 22; John 20, 17.]

Acts 2, 31. He [David], seeing this before, spake of the resurrection of Christ, that his soul was not left in hell [literally, *hades*, where he was, but was not left], neither his flesh did see corruption.

1 Pet. 3, 18. 19. For Christ also hath once suffered for sins, the just for the unjust, that he might bring us to God, being put to death in the flesh, but quickened by the spirit [literally, being put to death, indeed, in flesh, but quickened in spirit]: by which [spirit, or rational soul] also he went and preached unto the spirits [departed souls] in prison.

Eph. 4, 9. Now that he ascended, what is it but that he also descended first into the lower parts of the earth?

Comp. Ps. 16, 8; Acts 2, 27; Rom. 10, 7; Phil. 2, 10; 1 Pet. 4, 6.

5. *What comfort do you derive from Christ's descent into hades, or the region of the departed?*

Christ has delivered us from the terrors of hell, and opened the gate of heaven to all believers.

1 Cor. 15, 55, 57. O death, where is thy sting? O grave [or hades] where is thy victory?... Thanks be to God which giveth us the victory through our Lord Jesus Christ.

Luke 23, 43. And Jesus said unto him: Verily, I say unto thee, To-day thou shalt be with me in paradise.
Eph. 4, 8. He led captivity captive.—Comp. Col. 2, 15.
Rev. 1, 18. I have the keys of hell [hades] and of death.

NOTES AND HINTS.

The Hebrew word *Gehenna* is generally used in Scripture to denote the place of torment. The Hebrew word *Sheol* and the Greek *Hades* signify the grave and the place of departed spirits. Our English version translates *Hades* and *Gehenna* by the same word, "hell," and obliterates an important distinction between the realm of the dead and the place of torment.

XXX. The Resurrection, and Ascension of Christ.

1. *What does the Bible teach concerning the resurrection of Christ?*

On the third day after his crucifixion, Christ rose from the grave in his glorified body, as the conqueror of death, and the prince of life, and appeared repeatedly to his disciples.

The history of the resurrection and the manifestations of the risen Redeemer: Matt. 28; Mark 16; Luke 24; John 20 and 21; 1 Cor. 15, 1 ff.—Comp. also John 2, 19; 10, 17. 18, where the resurrection is represented as the act of his own divine power, which is identical with the power of the Father.

2. *What is the import of this event?*

By his resurrection, Christ completed the work of redemption, brought life and immortality to light, and gave us a sure pledge of our blessed resurrection.

* John 11, 25. I am the resurrection, and the life: he that believeth in me, though he were dead, yet shall he live.
John 14, 19. Because I live, ye shall live also.
* Rom. 4, 25. Jesus was delivered for our offences, and was raised again for our justification.

2 Tim. 1. 10. Jesus Christ hath abolished death, and hath brought life and immortality to light through the gospel.
Acts 2, 32–36; 4, 10–12; 5, 30. 31; Rom. 1, 4; 8, 11; Col. 2, 12. 13; 1 Cor 15, 20–22. 54–57; 1 Pet. 1, 3. 4; Job 19, 25.

3. *How should this faith move you?*

To arise from the sleep of sin, and to walk with Christ in newness of life.

* Eph. 5, 14. Awake, thou that sleepest, and arise from the dead, and Christ shall give thee light.
Rom. 6, 4. Like as Christ was raised up from the dead by the glory of the Father, even so we also should walk in newness of life.

4. *What is revealed concerning the ascension of Christ?*

Forty days after his resurrection, Christ ascended visibly to heaven from Mount Olivet, in presence of the apostles, and sat down at the right hand of God.

The history of the ascension, see Mark 16, 19; Luke 24, 50. 51; Acts 1, 3. 9–11.—Comp. John 14, 2. 3; Eph. 4, 8. 10; 1 Pet. 3, 22; Heb. 9, 24.

5. *Is Christ, then, absent from us?*

Certainly not; he is always invisibly present with his people by his word and Spirit, in the full power of his mediatorial life and work, even to the end of the world.

* Matt. 28, 20. Lo, I am with you alway, even unto the end of the world.
* Matt. 18, 20. Where two or three are gathered together in my name, there am I in the midst of them.
Eph. 1, 23. The church is his body, the fulness of him that filleth all in all.

6. *What should the ascension of Christ teach you?*

To seek those things which are above, so

that we may become partakers at last of his heavenly glory.

* Col. 3, 1. 2. If ye then be risen with Christ, seek those things which are above, where Christ sitteth on the right hand of God. Set your affection on things above, not on things on the earth.

Phil. 3, 20. Our conversation is in heaven, from whence also we look for the Saviour, the Lord Jesus Christ.

John 17, 24. Father, I will that they also, whom thou hast given me, be with me where I am; that they may behold my glory which thou hast given me.

XXXI. Christ's Sitting at the Right Hand of God, and His Return to Judgment.

1. *What do you mean by saying: "He sitteth at the right hand of God, the Father Almighty?"*

That Christ, as the God-man, has part in the eternal glory and almighty power of God.

Mark 16, 19. He was received up into heaven, and sat on the right hand of God.

* Matt. 28, 18. All power is given unto me in heaven and on earth.

1 Pet. 3, 22. Christ is gone into heaven, and is on the right hand of God; angels and authorities and powers being made subject unto him.

Matt. 26, 64; Eph. 1, 20–23; Phil. 2, 9; Heb. 1, 3; 12, 2.

2. *What is the work of Christ in heaven?*

He rules and keeps his Church as a mighty King, and he intercedes for us as a merciful High-priest.

1 Cor. 15, 25. Christ must reign, till he hath put all enemies under his feet.—Ps. 110, 1; Heb. 1, 13; Eph. 1, 20–23; Rev. 11, 15.

Rom. 8, 34. Christ is at the right hand of God, who also maketh intercession for us.—Heb. 7, 25; 1 John 2, 1.

Compare the next lesson.

3. *What comfort do you derive from this faith?*

That at all times, even in tribulation and persecution, we are sure of the almighty protection of our Saviour, who rules and overrules all things for our good, and will take us up at last to himself in heaven.

* John 16, 33. In the world ye shall have tribulation: but be of good cheer; I have overcome the world.
John 10, 28; Rom. 8, 28. 31-39; Rev. 3, 21.

4. *What does the Bible teach concerning the second coming of Christ?*

On the last day, Christ will appear in great power and glory, raise the dead, and judge the world in righteousness.

* Matt. 25, 31. 32. When the Son of man shall come in his glory, and all the holy angels with him, then shall he sit upon the throne of his glory; and before him shall be gathered all nations.—Comp. v. 32-46.
Acts 10, 42. Christ was ordained of God to be the judge of quick and dead.
Rev. 1, 7. Behold, he cometh with clouds; and every eye shall see him, and they also which pierced him: and all kindreds of the earth shall wail because of him.
Acts 17, 31. He will judge the world in righteousness.
Matt. 26, 64; John 5, 27-29; Acts 1, 11; 2 Cor. 5, 10; 1 Thess. 4, 16; 2 Tim. 4, 1; 2 Pet. 3, 10-13; 1 John 3, 2; Rev. 3, 3; 6, 16. 17; 20, 12.

5. *What will he judge?*

The thoughts, words, and deeds of men.

1 Cor. 4, 5. The Lord will bring to light the hidden things of darkness, and will make manifest the counsels of the hearts.
Matt. 12, 36. 37. Every idle word that men shall speak, they shall give account thereof in the day of judgment. For by thy words thou shalt be justified, and by thy words thou shalt be condemned.
Rom. 2, 6. God will render to every man according to his deeds.—Comp. Prov. 24, 12; Rev. 2, 23; 20, 12; 22, 12; 2 Cor. 5, 10.

6. *How will he hold judgment?*

He will separate the righteous from the wicked, bring to light all their works, and award everlasting life and everlasting punishment.

Matt. 25, 32. 33. He shall separate them one from another, as a shepherd divideth his sheep from the goats: and he shall set the sheep on his right hand, but the goats on the left.

Matt. 25, 46. And these [those on the left hand] shall go away into everlasting punishment: but the righteous into life eternal.

* 2 Cor. 5, 10. We must all appear before the judgment-seat of Christ; that every one may receive the things done in his body, according to that he hath done, whether it be good or bad.

John 5, 29. And they shall come forth; they that have done good, unto the resurrection of life; and they that have done evil, unto the resurrection of damnation.

7. *Do we know the time of the coming of Christ?*

No; God alone knows the day and the hour when the Son of man shall come.

* Matt. 24, 44. Therefore be ye also ready: for in such an hour as ye think not, the Son of man cometh.

Mark 13, 32. But of that day and that hour knoweth no man, no, not the angels which are in heaven, neither the Son [in the days of his humiliation], but the Father.

1 Thess. 5, 2. The Lord so cometh as a thief in the night [*i.e.* unexpectedly].

Luke 12, 40; 21, 34–36; 2 Pet. 3, 10; Rev. 3, 3; 16, 15.

8. *What should you do, therefore?*

We should watch, and always be ready for the great day of judgment.

* Matt. 25, 13. Watch, therefore, for ye know neither the day nor the hour wherein the Son of man cometh.

Luke 12, 37. Blessed are those servants, whom the Lord when he cometh shall find watching.

Mark 13, 33–37; Luke 12, 35–40; 21, 34–36, and the parable of the ten virgins, Matt. 25, 1–13.

9. *Need the pious be afraid of that day?*

No; to the ungodly it will indeed be a day of terror, but to the godly, a day of joy and complete redemption.

Luke 23, 30. Then shall they begin to say to the mountains: Fall on us! and to the hills: Cover us!—Comp. Rev. 6, 16. 17; v. 6.

Luke 21, 28. And when these things begin to come to pass, then look up, and lift up your heads; for your redemption draweth nigh.

Rev. 22, 20. He which testifieth these things saith: Surely I come quickly. Amen. Even so, come, Lord Jesus!

XXXII. The Threefold Office and Work of Christ.

1. *What are the three offices of Christ?*

He is our Prophet, Priest, and King.

2. *Were there such offices before Christ?*

Yes: there were prophets, priests, and kings in the Jewish economy, who were types and forerunners of Christ.

3. *How is Christ distinguished from them?*

Christ unites all these offices in himself, and is the last and perfect Prophet, Priest, and King of redeemed humanity, forever.

4. *What do you mean by the prophetical office of Christ?*

Christ is the light of the world, and the truth itself, and has fully revealed to us the will and counsel of God in his doctrine and by his example.

* John 8, 12. I am the light of the world: he that

followeth me shall not walk in darkness, but shall have the light of life.

* John 14, 6. I am the way, the truth, and the life: no man cometh unto the Father, but by me.

John 15, 15. All things that I have heard of my Father I have made known unto you.

Col. 2, 3. In Christ are hid all the treasures of wisdom and knowledge.

John 1, 18; 4, 14; 6, 14 (comp. Deut. 18, 18. 19); 17, 6; Matt. 7, 29; 11, 27.

5. *What belongs to his prophetical office?*

His doctrine, prophecies, and miracles.

6. *What do you mean by the priestly office of Christ?*

Christ has reconciled us to God forever by his own perfect sacrifice on the cross, and intercedes continually for us at the right hand of the Father, as our eternal High-priest.

Heb. 5, 6. Thou art a priest forever, after the order of Melchizedek. (Ps. 110, 4.)

* Heb. 10, 14. By one offering he hath perfected forever them that are sanctified.—Comp. Matt. 20, 28; Rom. 3, 24. 25; 5, 8; 8, 3; Gal. 3, 13; 2 Cor. 5, 21.

* 1 John 2, 1. If any man sin, we have an advocate with the Father, Jesus Christ the righteous: and he is the propitiation for our sins; and not for ours only, but also for the sins of the whole world.—Comp. Rom. 8, 34; Heb. 7, 24. 25; 9, 24.

Comp. also Lesson XXVIII.

7. *What do you mean by the kingly office of Christ?*

Christ is the head of his Church in heaven and on earth, ruling it by his word and Spirit, protecting it against all enemies, and directing all things for his glory and the good of his people.

* Luke 1, 33. And he shall reign over the house of Jacob forever; and of his kingdom there shall be no end.

1 Cor. 15, 25. He must reign, till he hath put all enemies under his feet.

Ps. 110, 1; John 18, 36. 37; Matt. 28, 18; Eph. 1, 22. 23; 4, 15; 5, 23 ("Christ is the head of the church"); Phil. 2, 11; Rom. 8, 28; 1 Pet. 3, 22; 2 Pet. 1, 11; Dan. 2, 44; 7, 14. 27; Rev. 11, 15.

NOTES AND HINTS.

Q. 4. A prophet is a divinely inspired and commissioned teacher who proclaims the secret counsel of God, and generally also foretells future events connected with his kingdom. Christ, however, did not only bear witness to the truth, but he is the *personal* truth itself. He alone could say: "I am the light of the world," "I am the truth." From the mouth of any other man—even Moses, or St. Paul—such a declaration would be at once set down as a certain indication either of madness or blasphemy.

Q. 5. The DOCTRINE of Christ is the self-manifestation of his person as *the* truth, a testimony concerning himself, and his relation to the Father and to the world, and the nature and laws of his kingdom.— Compare especially the Sermon on the Mount (the legislation of the New Testament from the mount of beatitudes), Matt. 5–7; the parables, Matt. 13; Luke 15, etc., and his parting discourses in John 13–17. All his words are *spirit* and *life.* John 6, 63.—The PROPHECIES of Christ relate to his passion, death, and resurrection, the sending of the Holy Spirit, the destruction of Jerusalem, and the final judgment.—Comp. Matt. 24 and 25; Luke 19; John 2, 19–22; 3, 14. 15; 14, 16; 15, 26; 16, 13. 14. As no man can penetrate the future, true prophecy presupposes divine inspiration, and thus attests the divine mission of the prophet. But Christ prophesied from his own intuition.—The MIRACLES of Christ are the natural manifestations of his wonderful divine-human person, which is the great central miracle in the history of the world. They are, therefore, often simply called his *works,* John 5, 36; 10, 37, etc.

They confirm his divine mission to an unbelieving world. Some of the miracles are the healing of demoniacs, the change of water into wine (John 2), the feeding of the five thousand (John 6), the raising of Lazarus (John 11), and the resurrection of Christ himself by his own power, which is the power of Almighty God.—Comp. John 2, 19; 10, 18.

Q. 6. The priests of the Old Testament were mediators between God and the Jewish people, who offered sacrifices for them, prayed for them, and blessed them, but only in a preparatory and typical sense: hence the repetition of the sacrifices from day to day. Christ is both priest and sacrifice in one, and he is both in a perfect sense, and not for the Jews only, but for the whole world.

XXXIII. Of the Holy Spirit.

1. *What do you believe concerning the Holy Spirit?*

I believe in the HOLY GHOST; the holy catholic Church, the communion of saints; the forgiveness of sins; the resurrection of the body, and the life everlasting.

OF THE HOLY SPIRIT.

2. *Is not the work of Christ sufficient for our salvation?*

Certainly it is; but it must be applied to our personal benefit by the Holy Spirit.

* 1 Cor. 12, 3. No man can say that Jesus is the Lord, but by the Holy Ghost.
* Rom. 8, 9. If any man have not the Spirit of Christ, he is none of his.
Gal. 4, 6. Because ye are sons, God hath sent forth the Spirit of his Son into your hearts, crying, Abba, Father.
Tit. 3, 5. 6. According to his mercy he saved us, by the washing of regeneration, and renewing of the Holy Ghost, which he shed on us abundantly.

3. *How is this done?*

The Holy Spirit testifies of Christ as the Saviour of sinners, unites us to him by faith, and makes us partakers of all his benefits.

* John 15, 26. When the Comforter is come, whom I will send unto you from the Father, even the Spirit of truth, which proceedeth from the Father, he shall testify of me.
John 14, 26. The Comforter, which is the Holy Ghost, ... shall teach you all things, and bring all things to your remembrance, whatsoever I have said unto you.
John 16, 13. 14. The Spirit of truth ... will guide you into all truth. ... He shall glorify me: for he shall receive of mine, and shall show it unto you.

4. *Who is the Holy Spirit?*

The third person in the Holy Trinity, proceeding from the Father, and the Son.

Matt. 28, 19; 2 Cor. 13, 13; 1 John 5, 7.—John 14, 26; 15, 26.—Comp. Lesson XV., Q. 3.

5. *Why do you believe in the Divinity of the Holy Spirit?*

Because the Bible makes him equal with the Father, and the Son, and ascribes to him divine names, attributes, works, and honors.

Matt. 28, 19; 2 Cor. 13, 13; 1 John 5, 7.—Comp. Lesson XV., Q. 3.

Acts 5, 3. 4 (where Peter declares a lie to the Holy Ghost, v. 3, to be a lie not unto men, but unto God, v. 4); 1 Cor. 3, 16; John 14, 16. 17. 26; 16, 13. 14; 1 Pet. 1, 2; 4, 14; Heb. 9, 14; 1 Cor. 2, 10. 11; 12, 11.

6. *What is the work or office of the Holy Spirit?*

The regeneration, sanctification and glorification of the redeemed.

John 3, 5. 6; Tit. 3, 5–7; 1 Cor. 6, 11; Eph. 3, 16; 5, 17. 19; Gal. 5, 22.—Comp. Lessons XXXVIII. and XXXIX.

7. *What does this mean?*

The Holy Spirit creates, preserves, promotes, and perfects the Christian life in the children of God.

8. *Was not the Holy Spirit active before Christ?*

Yes: The Spirit wrought in the creation, inspired the prophets, sanctified believers under the Jewish economy, and comforted them by the hope of future redemption.

Gen. 1, 2 (the Spirit of God moved upon the face of the waters); Ps. 33, 6 (by the breath or Spirit of his mouth); Job 33, 4 (the Spirit of God hath made me); Gen. 6, 3 (my Spirit shall not always strive with men); Ps. 51, 11 (take not thy Holy Spirit from me); 2 Sam. 23, 2 (the Spirit of the Lord spake by David); Isa. 48, 16; Luke 1, 67. 70; 1 Pet. 1, 10. 11 (the Spirit of Christ was in the prophets); 2 Pet. 1, 21 (they were moved by the Holy Ghost).

9. *How does He work in the new dispensation?*

As the Spirit of Jesus Christ, applying to us the fulness of the accomplished redemption, and making us children of God and heirs with Christ of life everlasting.

* Rom. 8, 15–17. Ye have not received the spirit of bondage again to fear; but ye have received the Spirit of adoption, whereby we cry, Abba, Father. The Spirit itself beareth witness with our spirit, that we are the children of God: and if children, then heirs; heirs of God, and joint heirs with Christ; if so be that we suffer with him, that we may be also glorified together.—Comp. Gal. 4, 5-7.

10. *When was the Holy Spirit poured out in this fulness upon the apostles?*

On the day of Pentecost, the fiftieth day after the resurrection of Christ.

Acts 2, 1-13. The outpouring of the Holy Spirit was promised in the Old Testament, Joel 2, 28. 29. 32: Isa. 32, 15; 44, 3. 4; Ezek. 36, 26. 27; and by Christ, John 7, 37-39; 14, 16; 15, 26; Luke 24, 49; Acts 1, 8.

11. *Was the effusion of the Spirit confined to the day of Pentecost?*

No: The Spirit works continually in the Church, through the means of grace, and dwells in all true believers as their guide and comforter.

John 14, 16. I will pray the Father, and he shall give you another Comforter, that he may abide with you forever; even the Spirit of truth, whom the world cannot receive.

John 14, 26. The Comforter ... shall teach you all things.

* 1 Cor. 3, 16. Know ye not that ye are the temple of God, and that the Spirit of God dwelleth in you?

1 Cor. 6, 19. Know ye not that your body is the temple of the Holy Ghost which is in you?

* Gal. 5, 22. The fruit of the Spirit is love, joy, peace, long-suffering, gentleness, goodness, faith, meekness, temperance.

Comp. John 16, 13. 14; Rom. 8, 9. 11. 15-17; Gal. 4, 6; 1 John 3, 24; 4, 13.

12. *How can you receive the precious gift of the Holy Spirit?*

By prayer, and the right use of the means of grace.

* Luke 11, 13. If ye, being evil, know how to give good gifts unto your children; how much more shall your heavenly Father give the Holy Spirit to them that ask him?

Acts 2, 38. Repent, and be baptized every one of you in the name of Jesus Christ for the remission of sins, and ye shall receive the gift of the Holy Ghost.

Acts 8, 15-17; 10, 44; Eph. 1, 17; Ps. 51, 11.

NOTES AND HINTS.

Q. 3. As the Son revealed and glorified the Father, so the Holy Ghost reveals and glorifies the Son and applies his work to believers. We can not come to the Father except through the Son, neither can we come to the Son without the Spirit, who enables us to know and embrace him as our Lord and Saviour.

Q. 4. The Holy Spirit is not only a divine *power* and *gift*, but also a divine PERSON, coeternal and coequal in substance and majesty with the Father and the Son. For he is co-ordinate with the Father and the Son, and yet distinguished from both (Matt. 28, 19; 2 Cor. 13, 13); he is called *another* Comforter (John 14, 26); he *speaks* (Matt. 10, 20; Mark 13, 11; Acts 8, 29; 1 Tim. 4, 1); he *teaches* (John 14, 26; 16, 13; 1 Cor. 2, 13; 1 John 2, 20. 27); he *testifies* or *bears witness* (John 15, 26; Acts 20, 23; Rom. 8, 16; 1 John 5, 6); he *searches* all things (1 Cor. 2, 10); he *forbids* (Acts 16, 6); he *presses* or *urges* (Acts 18, 5); he can be *grieved* (Eph. 4, 30), *belied* (Acts 5, 3), and *blasphemed* (Matt. 12, 31).

XXXIV. The Christian Church.

1. *Where does the Holy Spirit dwell and work?*

In the Christian Church and in all believers.

2. *What is the Christian Church?*

The communion of all believers in Christ the head.

The Church in its *general* sense (as distinct from a *local congregation*, see Notes) is figuratively defined in the New Testament as *the body of Christ* (*i.e.* an organic union of different members and functions, ruled by Christ the head, animated by his Spirit, and used by him as his organ), Rom. 12, 5; 1 Cor. 12, 27; Eph. 1, 22, and often in Paul's Epistles; *the flock* (*fold*) *of Christ*, John 10, 16; Acts 20, 28; *the bride of Christ* or *of the Lamb*, John 3, 29; 2 Cor. 11, 2; Eph. 5, 25–27; Rev. 19, 7; 21, 2–9; 22, 17; a *holy temple in the Lord*, and a *habitation of God through the Spirit*, Eph. 2, 21; the *house of God*, the pillar and ground of the truth, 1 Tim. 3, 15; a *chosen generation*, a *royal priesthood*, a *holy nation*, a *peculiar people*, 1 Pet. 2, 9; Tit. 2, 14. It is also called the *Church* (assembly, congregation) *of God* or *of Christ*, Acts 20, 28; 1 Cor. 10, 32; Eph. 5, 23; 1 Tim. 3, 15.

3. *Who founded the Christian Church?*

Our exalted Saviour, on the fiftieth day after

his resurrection, by the outpouring of the Holy Spirit upon his disciples, in Jerusalem.

Acts 2 gives the history of the birthday of the Church; the outpouring of the Spirit upon the apostles (which was both their *baptism* of fire and Spirit, and their *ordination*); the speaking with new tongues; the missionary sermon of Peter; the conversion and baptism of the three thousand (v. 47); the daily increase of the Church.—Although the Christian Church did not make its appearance as a distinct institution and society till the day of Pentecost, yet its foundations were laid previously by Christ's preaching on the kingdom of heaven, the call and commission of the apostles, and the institution of the sacraments of Baptism and the Lord's Supper.

* Matt. 16, 18. Upon this rock I will build my church; and the gates of hell [hades] shall not prevail against it.

Eph. 2, 20. Ye are built upon the foundation of the apostles and prophets, Jesus Christ himself being the chief cornerstone.

* 1 Cor. 3, 11. Other foundation can no man lay than that is laid, which is Jesus Christ.

4. *Can the Church ever perish?*

No: the gates of hell shall not prevail against Christ's Church.

Matt. 16, 18. [Hell, or rather *hades*, *i.e.* the empire of death, is here represented as a dreary prison with gates and bars, or as a hostile fortress, which in vain assails the immovable city of God.] Comp. also the seven thousand, 1 Kings 19, 18; Rom. 11, 2–5, who never bowed the knee to Baal. If the Jewish Church could not fail even in an age of prevailing idolatry, the Christian Church can still less fail.

5. *What are the essential attributes of the Church?*

The Church of Christ is one, holy, and universal in its nature and destination; and is to become so more and more in its manifestation.

1. *Unity*, John 10, 16 (there shall be *one fold*, and one shepherd); 17, 23 (where Christ prays that his disciples *may be made perfect in one*); Acts 2, 42; 4, 32 (actual unity of the Apostolic Church at Jerusalem); Eph. 4, 3–6 (the *unity of the Spirit* in the bond of peace, etc.); Rom. 12, 5 (we, being many, are *one body* in Christ, and every one members one of another).

2. *Holiness*, Eph. 5, 25–27 (*holy* and *without blemish*); 1 Cor.

3, 16. 17 (the temple of God is *holy*, which temple ye are); 6, 11; Col. 3, 9-12; Rom 6, 4; Gal. 2, 20; 1 Pet. 2, 9; Ps. 93, 5 (*holiness* becometh thine house, O Lord, forever).

3. *Universality* (catholicity), or destination for all nations and generations, Matt. 24, 14 (the gospel of the kingdom shall be preached in *all the world* for a witness unto *all nations*); 28, 19 (teach *all nations*); Rom. 11, 25. 26 (the *fulness of the Gentiles* shall come in, and *all Israel* shall be saved); Rev. 5, 9 out of every kindred, and tongue, and people, and nation).

6. *What is meant by the Church militant?*

The Church on earth, in conflict with the ungodly world, till the coming of Christ.

Matt. 10, 16-39 (Behold, I send you forth as sheep in the midst of wolves); John 16, 33 (in the world ye shall have tribulation); 1 Tim. 6, 12 (Fight the good fight of faith); 2 Tim. 4, 7. 8 (I have fought a good fight, etc.); Rev. 7, 14 (These are they which came out of great tribulation); Acts 14, 22 (we must through much tribulation enter into the kingdom of God).

7. *What is meant by the Church triumphant?*

The perfect kingdom of glory in heaven.

Isa. 60, 1-22; John 17, 24; Rev. 7, 9-17; 21 and 22; Heb. 12, 22. 23.

8. *What is the mission of the Church on earth?*

To bring unbelievers to Christ, and to prepare believers for heaven.

9. *Does external communion with the Church suffice to save us?*

No: we must be living members of the body of Christ.

Compare the distinction between the many who are *called*, and the few who are *chosen*, Matt. 22, 14; between the *fruitbearing*, and the *unfruitful* branches on the vine of Christ, John 15, 4-6; between those who merely *say:* Lord, Lord! and those who *do* the will of God, Matt. 7, 21; Luke 6, 46; between the *hearers*, and the *doers* of the word, Jam. 1, 22; Rom. 2, 13; between the vessels of *gold* and *silver*, and the vessels of *wood* and *earth*, in the same house of God, 2 Tim. 2, 20; between those who have only the *form* of godliness, and those who have the *power* thereof, 2 Tim. 3, 5.

10. *What will become at last of dead and hypocritical members of the Church?*
They will be cut off, and cast into the fire.

* Matt. 7, 19. Every tree that bringeth not forth good fruit is hewn down, and cast into the fire.

John 15, 6. If a man abide not in me, he is cast forth as a branch, and is withered; and men gather them, and cast them into the fire, and they are burned.

Compare the parable of the tares among the wheat, Matt. 13, 24–30; and the parable of the net, v. 47–50.

11. *What do you mean by the Communion of Saints?*
The true children of God in heaven and on earth are one in Christ, their common head and Saviour, and should manifest this unity by brotherly love and mutual intercession.

* John 10, 16. There shall be one fold, and one shepherd.

John 17, 23. I in them, and thou in me, that they may be made perfect in one.

Gal. 3, 28. There is neither Jew nor Greek [we may add, neither Greek nor Latin, neither Catholic nor Protestant, neither Lutheran nor Reformed, neither Episcopalian nor Presbyterian, etc.], there is neither bond nor free, there is neither male nor female: for ye are all one in Christ Jesus.

Eph. 4, 3–6. Endeavoring to keep the unity of the Spirit in the bond of peace. There is one body and one Spirit, even as ye are called in one hope of your calling; one Lord, one faith, one baptism, one God and Father of all, who is above all, and through all, and in you all.

Comp. John 13, 34. 35; Acts 4, 32; Rom. 12, 4–6; Eph. 4, 15. 16; 5, 30; 1 John 1, 3; 4, 20; 1 Pet. 1, 22; 4, 8–10; Heb. 13, 1.

NOTES AND HINTS.

Q. 1. The word *church* (from the Greek *Kuriakon, Kurios, Lord* = the Lord's house, the Lord's property) is the usual rendering, in our English version, for the Greek *ekklesia*, which means properly a popular assembly, convocation or congregation, and was first used in a secular sense (see Acts 19, 39), then applied to a religious assembly, called out of the world by the gospel. It signifies in the New Testament either the *Church universal* (Matt. 16, 18; 1 Cor. 12, 28; Gal. 1, 13; Eph. 1, 22; 1 Tim. 3, 15, and wherever it is called the *body of Christ,* the *bride of Christ,* the *temple of God,* etc.), or a *particular congrega-*

THE CHRISTIAN CHURCH.

tion (as in Jerusalem, Acts 8, 1; 11, 22; in Antioch, 11, 26; in Corinth, 1 Cor. 1, 2; 2 Cor. 2, 1; in Thessalonica, 1 Thess. 1, 1; 2 Thess. 1, 1; at Cenchreæ, Rom. 16, 1; in the house of Philemon. v. 2; of Aquila and Priscilla at Rome, Rom. 16, 5; the churches among the Gentiles, Rom. 16, 4, of Asia Minor, 1 Cor. 16, 19, of Galatia, Gal. 1, 2; the seven churches in Asia, Rev. 1, 4. 11. 20). The Saviour himself uses the term church (*ekklesia*) twice,—once (Matt. 16, 18) in the general, and once (Matt. 18, 17) in the particular sense. In this lesson it always means the Church proper or universal, as in the Creed. The Church universal only (and no particular congregation, or even denomination) is an article of faith; yet not in the same high sense as God is. Hence the Creed (as is noticed by some ancient fathers, and even by the Roman Catechism) here changes the language by leaving out the preposition *in* and substituting the mere accusative. We believe *in* God the Father, *in* Christ, and *in* the Holy Ghost, but we believe *the* holy catholic Church, which is a creature of God, and an organ of Christ. So also we believe (not *in*, but simply) the forgiveness of sins, the resurrection of the body, and the life everlasting.—Besides these two *scriptural* significations, the term *church* is also applied, in ecclesiastical usage, to the church-*building*, or *house* of worship, and to a *confession* or *denomination*, as when we speak of the Greek, Latin, Lutheran, Reformed, Churches, etc.

Q. 4. Particular congregations and entire denominations may pass away, but the Church universal is imperishable, and will only change its form and condition, but not its essence, at the second coming of Christ. It will then pass from the militant into the triumphant stage. It will cease as a *pædagogical institution* or *training-school* for heaven, but it will continue forever as the *communion of saints*, and as *the perfect kingdom of God*.

Q. 5. The Apostles' Creed mentions only *holiness* and *catholicity* (*sanctam ecclesiam catholicam*), the Nicene Creed (A.D. 325 and 381) more fully *unity, holiness, catholicity,* and *apostolicity* (*unam, sanctam, catholicam et apostolicam ecclesiam*), as essential attributes of the Church of Christ. These belong to it by virtue of its union with Christ, because he is *one* and has founded but one Church by his apostles and rules it as the head; because he is *holy*, and has purged the Church by his own blood and consecrated it to God and called it to holiness; and because he is the Saviour of the *whole world*, and by his servants calls all nations, generations, and classes of men into his kingdom. But these attributes are only imperfectly actualized in the Church *militant* on *earth*, and will not fully appear till the glorious coming of Christ. Many divisions mar the unity, many corruptions obscure the holiness, of the Church; and, notwithstanding its inherent universality, the greater part of the human race is not even Christianized. What the apostle says of himself, that he bears the heavenly treasure in earthen vessels (2 Cor. 4, 7), that he has not yet attained to perfection (Phil. 3. 12), and that it doth not yet appear what we shall be (1 John 3, 2), is true also of the whole body of believers in the present state. The Church is represented as *growing* gradually, like a grain of mustard-seed (Matt. 13, 32), or like a body (Eph. 4, 13. 16), unto the measure of the stature of the fulness of Christ. The unity, holiness, and catholicity of the Church are articles of faith, and really at hand, if we look to Christ and the inherent power and capacity of his kingdom; but they are also articles of hope and of duty, to be realized more and more fully by the prayers and activity of the Church under its divine Head.

Q. 6 and 7. The Church *militant* and the Church *triumphant* are not two different Churches, but two *states* and *periods* of the same Church, divided by the coming of Christ. They may be compared to the state of humiliation and the state of exaltation in the life of Christ (comp. Lesson

XXV.); yet with this difference,—that the Saviour was free from sin and error even in his state of humiliation, which cannot be said of any branch or period of the catholic Church on earth, where good and bad are mixed, and will be till the final judgment (comp. Matt. 13, 24–30; 47–50). Sometimes the distinction is understood of two coexisting *branches* of the Church, namely, the Church of the living on earth, and the Church of the departed saints (and angels) in heaven. But the full and final triumph does not appear, at all events, before the coming of Christ and the general resurrection.

Q. 9. The difference between *true* or inward, and mere *nominal* or outward church-membership has given rise, since the Reformation, to the distinction between the *invisible* and the *visible* Church. By this we are not to understand two distinct churches, but the invisible Church is *in* the visible, as the soul is in the body or as the kernel is in the shell. Both together constitute the full conception of the Church in the general sense of the term as used in the Bible. The invisible Church consists of all the true children of God; the visible, of all professors, or all who call themselves Christians. The invisible Church coincides with the *kingdom of God*, or *of heaven*, which is within us (comp. Luke 17, 21; Rom. 14, 17), and which forms the inward and abiding essence of the Church. It may be called invisible, because it is within us, because its head, Christ, is invisible, and because God alone infallibly knows his own (John 10, 14; 2 Tim. 2, 19). Nevertheless, the invisible Church is also visible both as to its members and as to its ordinances and institutions. True faith must manifest itself in confession and good works. The Church is compared to a city set on a hill, which *cannot be hid* (Matt. 5, 14), and is frequently called the *body* of Christ (eight times in the Epistle to the Ephesians alone). Hence the terms *visible* and *invisible* (also *real* and *ideal*, *mixed* and *pure*) are liable to misunderstanding. It is better to adhere to the scriptural terminology and distinction between the *church*, and the *kingdom of heaven*. For the pupil, it is enough to know the practical bearing of the distinction upon the individual, as brought out in the question and answer.

XXXV. The Means of Grace.

1. *How does the Holy Spirit work in the Church?*

By the means of grace.

2. *What are the principal means of grace?*

The Word of God, and the Sacraments.

3. *How are these related to each other?*

By the word of God salvation is preached to us; by the sacraments it is signed and sealed to us.

THE MEANS OF GRACE.

4. *What is the word of God?*

The revealed truth of God, which is taught in the Holy Scriptures, and continually proclaimed by the preaching of the gospel.

John 17, 17. Sanctify them through thy truth: thy word is truth.

Rom. 10, 17. Faith cometh by hearing [or, preaching], and hearing by the word of God.

1 Pet. 1, 23. This is the word which by the gospel is preached unto you.

Heb. 4, 12. The word of God is quick, and powerful, and sharper than any two-edged sword, piercing even to the dividing asunder of soul and spirit, and of the joints and marrow, and is a discerner of the thoughts and intents of the heart.

Comp. Heb. 4, 2; James 1, 18, and Lessons III–VI.

5. *Who instituted the preaching of the gospel?*

Jesus Christ, when he sent out the apostles with the commission: "Preach the gospel to every creature."

Mark 16, 15. And he said unto them: Go ye into all the world, and preach the gospel to every creature.

Matt. 28, 19. Go ye, therefore, and teach all nations.

Eph. 4, 11. 12. He gave some, apostles; and some, prophets; and some, evangelists; and some, pastors and teachers; for the perfecting of the saints, for the work of the ministry, for the edifying of the body of Christ.

1 Cor. 4, 1. 2; 2 Cor. 5, 18–20; 1 Tim. 3, 1. ff.

6. *What is a sacrament?*

A holy ordinance instituted by Christ, whereby, under visible signs and seals, divine grace is offered and applied to believers.

Rom. 4, 11. Abraham received the sign of circumcision, a seal of the righteousness of the faith which he had yet being uncircumcised.

7. *What are the typical sacraments of the Old Testament?*

Circumcision, and the Passover.

Gen. 17, 7-13; Rom. 4, 11.—Ex. 12, 2. ff; 1 Cor. 5, 7.—Comp. Col. 2, 17; Heb. 10, 1.

8. *What are the sacraments of the New Testament?*

Holy Baptism, and the Holy Communion or the Lord's Supper.

1 John 5, 6. This is he that came by water and blood, even Jesus Christ; not by water only, but by water and blood. And it is the Spirit that beareth witness, because the Spirit is truth.

9. *How are these two sacraments related to each other?*

By Baptism we are introduced into communion with Christ; by the Lord's Supper we are preserved and strengthened in it.

10. *What is the effect of the sacraments?*

They convey a blessing to the worthy, a curse to the unworthy, partaker.

1 Cor. 11, 29.

11. *What is necessary for the worthy reception of a sacrament?*

Sincere repentance of our sins, and a hearty faith in Christ.

12. *Are the sacraments necessary to salvation?*

No: we are bound to the ordinances of God, but God is free.

Comp. John 3, 8.

NOTES AND HINTS.

Q. 1 and 2. The Spirit of God works also through *prayer, praise, Providence* and other ways. But the Word and the Sacraments are more particularly called the means of grace in theology. On *Prayer* the Catechism treats in the first part, hence it is here omitted.

Q. 6. What is said of circumcision, Rom. 4, 11, is justly applied to Baptism, the corresponding sacrament of the New Testament.

According to the doctrine of the evangelical churches, three things are necessary to constitute a sacrament; (1) an outward sign or natural element (as water in Baptism, and bread and wine in the Holy Communion); (2) an inward grace or divine promise (as the remission of sins, communion with Christ); (3) divine institution by Christ, with his express command to observe such a rite (as: "Baptize all nations," and, "Do this in remembrance of me").

Q. 8. The Greek and Roman Churches have, besides Baptism and the Lord's Supper, five other sacraments, which, however, are wanting in one or the other of the three marks mentioned in the preceding note,—especially the express commandment of Christ. These are *Confirmation*, *Penance* (confession to, and absolution by, the priest), *Matrimony*, *Holy Orders* (ordination of priests), and *Extreme Unction*. We must make a distinction between sacraments proper (Baptism and the Holy Communion), and sacramental acts or sacred rites (confirmation, marriage, and ordination).

Q. 9. Baptism has been called the *sacrament of regeneration* (or washing of regeneration, Tit. 3, 5); the Holy Communion, the *sacrament of sanctification*. The former marks the beginning, the latter the progress, of Christian life; the one corresponds to the birth, the other to the growth and nourishment, of the natural life. Hence Baptism cannot be repeated (once baptized, always baptized); while the use of the Lord's Supper can and should be repeated.

Q. 11. Faith does not *produce* the sacramental blessing, which is inherent in the divine promise and ordinance, but it is necessary to *receive* and to *apply* it; as the hand and the mouth receive the food which contains the nourishing power, but which would be of no avail to us without the organ that applies it.

Q. 12. The general necessity of Baptism to salvation is based upon Mark 16, 16 and John 3, 5; but it has always been restricted in the Church by the correct principle that not the *want* but the *contempt* of the ordinance condemns. According to the word of Christ, Mark 16, 16, faith and Baptism save, but unbelief only (not the want of Baptism) condemns. The penitent thief on the cross, who died before he had an opportunity to be baptized, was promised a place in paradise (Luke 23, 43). Cornelius received the Holy Spirit before he was baptized by Peter (Acts 10, 44–48). The apostles, with the exception of Paul, only received the preparatory water-baptism of John, which still belonged to the Jewish dispensation, and their baptism of fire and of the Spirit on the day of Pentecost took the place of Christian water-baptism; for this they could only have received from Christ, who did not baptize (John 4, 2). In the ancient Church, the bloody baptism of martyrdom was regarded as an equivalent for water-baptism. The salvation of *all children* who die in infancy is not indeed, an article of revealed *faith* and public *doctrine*, but may be entertained as an article of Christian *hope* and *charity*, based upon a wide interpretation and general application of the precious words of Christ concerning the children which were brought to him, "Of such is the kingdom of heaven," Matt. 19, 14; Mark 10, 14. But they, too, must first experience regeneration, as the indispensable condition of entering into the kingdom of God, John 3, 5, and the merits of Christ, out of whom there can be no salvation, must be applied to them in some way. If all infants be saved, the greater part of mankind would be saved; for more than one-half die in infancy. A consoling thought! But, on the other hand, we must be equally careful not to undervalue the ordinances. While God is above all rules, we are bound to his revealed way of salvation, and cannot wilfully neglect the ordinary and regular means of grace without great danger to our souls.

XXXVI. Holy Baptism.

1. *When did Christ institute holy Baptism?*

After his resurrection, and shortly before his ascension.

2. *By what words?*

TEACH ALL NATIONS, BAPTIZING THEM IN THE NAME OF THE FATHER, AND OF THE SON, AND OF THE HOLY GHOST; TEACHING THEM TO OBSERVE ALL THINGS WHATSOEVER I HAVE COMMANDED YOU.

Matt. 28, 19. 20; Mark 16, 16.

3. *What is the outward sign in Baptism?*

Water, by which the purifying and renewing power of the Holy Spirit is represented.

Eph. 5, 26. That he might sanctify and cleanse it [the Church] with the washing of water by the word.
John 3, 5; Tit. 3, 5; Heb. 10, 22.

4. *What inward grace and spiritual benefit are signified by Baptism?*

The remission of sins, and the gift of the Holy Spirit.

* Mark 16, 16. He that believeth and is baptized, shall be saved; but he that believeth not, shall be damned.

Acts 2, 38. Repent, and be baptized every one of you in the name of Jesus Christ for the remission of sins, and ye shall receive the gift of the Holy Ghost.

Gal. 3, 27. As many of you as have been baptized into Christ, have put on Christ.

Tit. 3, 5. According to his mercy he saved us, by the washing of regeneration, and renewing of the Holy Ghost.

Rom. 6, 3. 4. Know ye not, that so many of us as were baptized into Jesus Christ, were baptized into his death? Therefore we are buried with him by baptism into death: that like as

HOLY BAPTISM.

Christ was raised up from the dead by the glory of the Father, even so we also should walk in newness of life.
John 3, 5; Eph. 5, 26; Acts 22, 16.

5. *What, then, is the nature of Baptism?*

Baptism is a covenant of grace of the triune God with man, in which God promises forgiveness and salvation, and man vows obedience and devotion to him.

1 Pet. 3, 21. The like figure whereunto even baptism doth also now save us, not the putting away of the filth of the flesh, but the answer [or, stipulation] of a good conscience toward God.

Matt. 28, 20. Teaching them to observe all things whatsoever I have commanded you.

* Isa. 54, 10. The mountains shall depart, and the hills be removed; but my kindness shall not depart from thee, neither shall the covenant of my peace be removed, saith the Lord that hath mercy on thee.

6. *Will, then, all baptized persons be saved?*

No; but those only who keep their baptismal vow and are faithful unto death.

* Rev. 2, 10. Be thou faithful unto death, and I will give thee a crown of life.

Matt. 24, 13. He that shall endure unto the end, the same shall be saved.

Matt. 20, 16; James 1, 12; 2 Tim. 2, 11. 12; 4, 6–10; Rev. 3, 11. 15. 16. Examples of unfaithfulness and hypocrisy: Ananias, and Simon Magus, Acts 5 and 8.

7. *What is the consequence if we neglect our part of the baptismal covenant?*

We forfeit its benefits and increase our guilt.

EXAMPLES of unfaithfulness and hypocrisy: Ananias and Sapphira, Acts 5; and Simon Magus, Acts 8.

8. *Is there forgiveness for sins committed after Baptism?*

Yes: if we sincerely repent and take refuge in Christ.

*1 John 1, 8. 9. If we say that we have no sin, we deceive ourselves, and the truth is not in us. If we confess our sins, he is faithful and just to forgive us our sins, and to cleanse us from all unrighteousness.

1 John 2, 1. If any man sin, we have an advocate with the Father, Jesus Christ the righteous.

9. *What is the duty of those baptized?*

They should evermore be thankful to God for receiving them into his covenant of grace, and never doubt his promises; but they should also renew their vows by daily repentance, and grow up to full manhood in Christ.

NOTES AND HINTS.

Q. 2. The literal version of the great commission, Matt. 28, 19. 20, reads; "Go ye, therefore, and *make disciples* [*i. e.* true believers or Christians] of all nations, by *baptizing* them *into* the name..., by *teaching* them"... Baptism and instruction are specified as the two means by which all nations should be converted to Christianity. The "*into* the name" is more than, *with reference to,* or *by authority of* (as "*in* the name," after the Vulgate: "*in nomine*"), and seems to express the idea of introduction into fellowship and communion with the triune God and consecration to his service and praise. In other passages the Common Version has more accurately translated, baptize *into* Christ. Rom. 6, 3, 4; Gal. 3, 27.

Q. 3. Water is essential to the sacrament of Baptism. But the questions as to the *quality* (warm or cold, rain-, spring-, or river-water), the *quantity,* and the *mode* of its application are points upon which Christians differ.

There have been many warm disputes about the proper *mode* and *subjects* of baptism, the right of *infant* baptism, the validity of *heretical* baptism, the rite of *confirmation,* and the *terms* of full admission to church membership. These questions lie beyond the proper sphere of a Sunday-school Catechism. The Baptists reject infant baptism and insist upon immersion as the only proper mode of baptism; the other Protestant, as well as the Greek and Latin churches, hold to infant baptism as a primitive custom, and on the ground that the covenant embraces children of pious parents as well as adults; but it requires the presence of Christian family life and the guarantee of Christian nurture. Confirmation of the baptized is practised in the Protestant Episcopal, Lutheran, and German Reformed churches, and is preceded by a course of catechetical instruction. In other Protestant churches those only are received into full communion, who give evidence of conversion.

XXXVII. The Lord's Supper.

1. *What is the second sacrament of the Christian Church?*

The Lord's Supper or the Holy Communion.

2. *When did Christ institute this sacrament?*

In the night before his crucifixion.

3. *Give an account of its institution.*

Our Lord Jesus, the same night in which He was betrayed, took bread; and when He had given thanks, He brake it, and said:

Take, eat: this is My body, which is broken for you: this do in remembrance of Me.

After the same manner also He took the cup, when He had supped, saying:

Drink ye all of it: this cup is the new testament in My blood, which is shed for many for the remission of sins: this do ye, as oft as ye drink it, in remembrance of me.

Matt. 26, 26–28; Mark 14, 22–24; Luke 22, 19. 20; 1 Cor. 11, 23–25. (We have taken the text from St. Paul, but added from St. Matthew the words:
"Drink ye all of it," and, "which is shed for many for the remission of sins.")

4. *What are the visible signs or elements of the Lord's Supper?*

Bread and wine, by which the body and blood of Christ are set forth and sealed.

5. *What is the invisible grace of the Lord's Supper?*

The communion of the body and blood of Christ, who died for us and lives forever.

The words of institution: "This is my body.... This is my blood." See Q. 3. 1 Cor. 10, 16.

6. *What is the meaning and design of this sacrament?*

It is a memorial of the blessed sacrifice of Christ, whereby we commemorate his passion and death, and appropriate anew the benefits of his atonement.

* Luke 22, 19. This do in remembrance of me.
1 Cor. 11, 26. As often as ye eat this bread, and drink this cup, ye do shew [or, shew ye] the Lord's death till he come.

7. *What else is this sacrament?*

A communion of the body and blood of Christ, whereby the souls of believers are nourished unto everlasting life.

* 1 Cor. 10, 16. The cup of blessing which we bless, is it not the communion of the blood of Christ? The bread which we break, is it not the communion of the body of Christ?
John 6, 56. He that eateth my flesh and drinketh my blood, dwelleth in me, and I in him.
Eph. 5, 30. We are members of his body, of his flesh, and of his bones.
Compare the whole section, John 6, 51-58, the parable of the vine and the branches, 15, 1-9, and the parting discourses of our Saviour immediately before and after the institution of this sacred ordinance, chapters 13-17.

8. *What is it in addition to this?*

A communion of believers with each other. as members of the same mystical body of Christ.

* 1 Cor. 10, 17. For we being many are one bread and one body: for we are all partakers of that one bread.
Comp. John 13, 34. 35; 15, 12; Rom. 12, 5; 1 John 1, 3.

9. *What, then, does the believer receive in the Lord's Supper?*

Jesus Christ, who is the bread of life, together with all his benefits.

* John 6, 51. I am the living bread which came down from heaven: if any man eat of this bread, he shall live forever; and the bread that I will give, is my flesh, which I will give for the life of the world.
John 6, 47–58; 1 Cor. 10, 16, and the words of institution, Q. 3.

10. *How do we receive this great blessing?*

Not after a natural or carnal manner, but through faith, by the power of the Holy Spirit, who unites us to Christ.

* John 6, 63. It is the spirit that quickeneth; the flesh profiteth nothing: the words that I speak unto you, they are spirit, and they are life.
2 Cor. 3, 6. The letter killeth, but the spirit giveth life.
John 6, 47. He that believeth on me hath everlasting life. —Comp. v. 54. Whoso eateth my flesh and drinketh my blood, hath eternal life; and I will raise him up at the last day.

11. *Who are invited to the Lord's Supper?*

All believers who heartily repent of their sins, repose their whole trust in Christ, and hunger and thirst after communion with him.

* Matt. 11, 28. Come unto me, all ye that labor and are heavy laden, and I will give you rest.
Matt. 5, 6. Blessed are they which do hunger and thirst after righteousness: for they shall be filled.
John 6, 37. Him that cometh to me, I will in no wise cast out.

12. *What do unworthy communicants receive in the Lord's Supper?*

They eat and drink judgment to themselves, not discerning the Lord's body.
1 Cor. 11, 27. 29.

13. *Should those guilty of gross offences be admitted to the Lord's Supper?*

By no means; but they should be suspended, or even be cut off from the Church, until they repent.
Matt. 18, 17; 2 Thess. 3, 6; 1 Cor. 5, 2; 2 Cor. 2, 6–8.

14. *How should we prepare ourselves for a worthy communion?*

By prayer, by meditation on Christ's passion, and by earnest self-examination as to our repentance, faith, love to Christ, to the brethren, and to all men.

* 1 Cor. 11, 28. Let a man examine himself, and so let him eat of that bread, and drink of that cup.
2 Cor. 13, 5. Examine yourselves, whether ye be in the faith; prove your own selves.
Comp. 1 Cor. 5, 7. 8; Matt. 5, 23. 24.

NOTES AND HINTS.

Q. 1. *Biblical* names: THE LORD'S SUPPER, 1 Cor. 11, 20, or THE LORD'S TABLE, 1 Cor. 10, 21, because the Lord instituted it, and offers himself as spiritual food; THE BREAKING OF BREAD, Acts 2, 42; comp. 1 Cor. 10, 16. *Later* names: THE HOLY COMMUNION, with reference to 1 Cor. 10, 16, 17, *i.e.* the celebration of the union of believers with Christ and among themselves; THE EUCHARIST, or thank-offering, because it is a commemoration of all the blessings of God, which culminate in redemption by the blood of Christ; also the sacrament of the ALTAR (comp. Heb. 13, 10), as a celebration of the atoning sacrifice of Christ before the altar.

The Lord's Supper took the place of the Jewish passover. Comp. 1 Cor. 5, 7. It is the inmost sanctuary, the holy of holies, of Christian worship, and its celebration is the nearest approach we can make to Christ in this world.

Q. 7. Hence the name *the holy communion* for this sacrament (1 Cor. 10, 16). This implies, however, both the communion of believers with Christ, their common head, and the communion of believers among themselves as members of the same body. The latter is the necessary fruit of the former, as love to our neighbor flows from love to God.

Q. 10. The passage John 6, 63 furnishes the key to the interpretation of the preceding section, v. 51–58, and the words of Christ generally, which are spirit and life, and should be understood accordingly. It excludes all those theories on the Lord's Supper which either carnalize and materialize it, or which resolve it into a mere symbol or figure and empty it of its profound spiritual mystery.

Q. 12. *Judgment*, or *punishment*, is the proper translation of the Greek *krima* in 1 Cor. 11, 29. The Common Version renders the word here, as also in Rom. 13, 2 and some other passages, by *damnation*, which had originally the same meaning, but is now restricted to the final and eternal *condemnation* (*katakrima*) of the wicked.

Q. 13. The Church may excommunicate a person for gross sin, or heresy, by the right of *discipline*. This is also called the *power of the keys*, by which the gates of the kingdom of heaven are opened to the penitent, and closed against the impenitent. Christ alone possesses this power, but he conferred it on Peter, Matt. 16, 18, and the apostles generally, Matt. 18, 18; John 20, 23, as his executive organs, and through the apostles on the Church at large. According to Matt. 18, 15–17, discipline has three degrees: (1) private admonition; (2) public admonition before the congregation; (3) excommunication, or exclusion from the Church and the use of the sacraments, by the joint act of the pastor and the congregation or its proper representatives. But this exclusion is only temporary, and looks to the repentance of the offender, after which he may and ought to be restored to the communion of the Church. Comp. 2 Cor. 2, 6–8.

Terrible examples of church discipline: Ananias and Sapphira, for lying and hypocrisy, Acts 5, 1–10; a member of the congregation of Corinth, for incest, 1 Cor. 5, 1–5; 2 Cor. 7, 12; and Hymeneus and Alexander, for pernicious heresy, 1 Tim. 1, 20; 2 Tim. 2, 17.

Q. 14. The *worthy* communicant is not one who considers himself worthy, but one who with the deep sense of his own *unworthiness* unites sincere faith in Christ's mercy. "The sacrifices of God are a broken spirit: a broken and a contrite heart, O God, thou wilt not despise" (Ps. 51, 17). Comp. Q. 11

XXXVIII. The Order of Salvation.—Regeneration.

1. *What are the principal acts in the work of grace?*

Election, vocation, regeneration, justification, sanctification, and glorification.

Rom. 8, 29. 30. Whom he did foreknow, he also did predestinate to be conformed to the image of his Son, that he might be the firstborn among many brethren. Moreover, whom he did predestinate, them he also called; and whom he called, them he also justified; and whom he justified, them he also glorified.

1 Cor. 1, 30. Christ is made unto us wisdom, and righteousness, and sanctification, and redemption.

2. *Wherein consists God's purpose of salvation?*

In that God, of his free grace, from eternity has chosen his children in Christ, that they should be holy and obtain salvation through him.

* 2 Thess. 2. 13. God hath from the beginning chosen you to salvation through sanctification of the Spirit and belief of the truth.

Eph. 1, 4. 5. According as he hath chosen us in him before the foundation of the world, that we should be holy and without blame before him in love: having predestinated us unto the adoption of children by Jesus Christ to himself, according to the good pleasure of his will.

1 Thess. 5, 9. God hath not appointed us to wrath, but to obtain salvation by our Lord Jesus Christ.

Comp. Rom. 8, 29; 9, 16; 2 Tim. 1, 9; 1 Pet. 1, 2. 20; Acts 13, 48; 15, 18; John 15, 16; Rev. 13, 8; 17, 8.

3. *What use should you make of this doctrine?*

It should increase our gratitude to God, make us more diligent and watchful in our conflict with sin, and give us comfort in our trials.

* 2 Pet. 1, 10. Give diligence to make your calling and election sure: for if ye do these things, ye shall never fall.

1 Cor. 10, 12. Let him that thinketh he standeth, take heed lest he fall.

Comp., for *warning*, Matt. 26, 41; John 8, 31; Rom. 11, 20–22; 1 Thess. 5, 6; Eph. 6, 18; 2 Pet. 3, 17;—for *comfort*, John 10, 27–29; Rom. 8, 35–39; 1 Pet. 1, 5; 2 Tim. 2, 19.

4. *What is vocation, or calling?*

The invitation given to the sinner, through the gospel, to enter into the kingdom of God.

* Rev. 3, 20. Behold, I stand at the door and knock: if any man hear my voice, and open the door, I will come in to him, and will sup with him, and he with me.

1 Thess. 2, 12. God hath called you unto his kingdom and glory.

2 Thess. 2, 14. He called you by our gospel.

Rom. 8, 30; 1 Cor. 1, 9; 1 Thess. 5, 24; 1 Pet. 2, 9 (who

THE ORDER OF SALVATION.

hath called you out of darkness into his marvellous light); Matt. 11, 28–30 (Come unto me, etc).—Comp. the parable of the great Supper, Luke 14, 16–24; Matt. 22, 1–14.

5. *What is conversion?*

Conversion is a change of heart, by which we turn away from sin and turn to Christ, in true repentance and faith.

Matt. 4, 17. Repent ye [change your mind]: for the kingdom of heaven is at hand.—[The beginning of Christ's preaching, as it was also that of John the Baptist, 3, 2.]

Matt. 18, 3. Except ye be converted, and become as little children, ye shall not enter into the kingdom of heaven.

* Acts 3, 19. Repent, and be converted, that your sins may be blotted out.

Acts 17, 30. God commandeth all men everywhere to repent.

Eph. 5, 14. Awake, thou that sleepest, and arise from the dead, and Christ shall give thee light.

Acts 26, 17. 18. 20 (that they should repent and turn to God); Rom. 13, 11. 12; 1 Cor. 15, 34; 2 Pet. 3, 9; 2 Cor. 7, 10 (repentance to salvation); Eph. 4, 22–24 (putting off the *old* man, and putting on the *new* man).

Examples: The prodigal son in the parable, Luke 15, 18–21; the three thousand on the day of Pentecost, Acts 2, 41; St. Paul, 9, 1–9; Cornelius, 10, 1 ff.; Lydia and the jailer at Philippi, 16, 14. 31, etc.

6. *What are the marks of true repentance?*

A sense of sin, hearty sorrow for it, hatred of it, and a sincere purpose to lead a life of holy obedience.

* 2 Cor. 7, 10. Godly sorrow worketh repentance to salvation not to be repented of: but the sorrow of the world worketh death.

Comp. Jer. 3, 13 (Acknowledge thine iniquity); Ps. 51, 3 (I acknowledge my transgressions); Matt. 5, 4 (Blessed are they that mourn); Luke 18, 13 (God be merciful to me a sinner); Matt. 3, 8 (Bring forth fruits meet for repentance).

EXAMPLES of *true* repentance, or *godly* sorrow to life: the sinful woman (Mary Magdalene), Luke 7, 36–48; comp. 8, 2; Zaccheus, Luke 19, 1–10; the prodigal son in the parable, 15, 18–21; the publican in the temple, 18, 13; the penitent thief on the cross, Luke 23, 40–43. True repentance for sins *after* conversion is shown by David, Ps. 51, and by Peter after denying his Saviour, Matt. 26, 75.

118 THE ORDER OF SALVATION.

EXAMPLES of *false* repentance, or *worldly* sorrow to death, which merely shrinks in horror from the terrible *effects* of sin, and despairs of the mercy of God: Cain, Gen. 4, 13; Pharaoh, Exod. 10, 16. 17; Saul, 1 Sam. 15, 30; Ahab, 1 Kings 21, 25. 29, and Judas, Matt. 27, 3 ff.

7. *What are the marks of true faith?*

Knowledge of Christ, assent to the truth of his gospel, and hearty trust in him as our Saviour.

Comp. Lesson XII.

8. *Can you repent and believe in your own strength?*

By no means; but only by the power of the Holy Spirit, who enlightens our darkened understanding, and creates in us a new heart.

* Jer. 31, 18. Turn thou me, and I shall be turned [converted].

Ps. 51, 10. Create in me a clean heart, O God; and renew a right spirit within me.

Ezek. 36, 26. A new heart also will I give you, and a new spirit will I put within you: and I will take away the stony heart out of your flesh, and I will give you a heart of flesh.

* Phil. 2, 13. It is God which worketh in you both to will and to do of his good pleasure.

Comp. Lam. 5, 21; John 6, 44; Luke 24, 45 (He opened their understanding); Acts 16, 14 (The Lord opened the heart of Lydia); 2 Tim. 2, 25 (if God will *give* them repentance); Acts 5, 31; 11, 18 (God *granted* repentance unto life).

9. *What do you call this great change?*

Regeneration or the new birth, without which no man can enter into the kingdom of God.

* John 3, 5. Except a man be born of water and of the Spirit, he cannot enter into the kingdom of God.—Comp. v. 3 and 8.

Tit. 3, 5. According to his mercy he saved us, by the washing of regeneration, and renewing of the Holy Ghost.

Eph. 2, 5. When we were dead in sins, God hath quickened us together with Christ.

1 Pet. 1, 23. Being born again, not of corruptible seed, but of incorruptible, by the word of God, which liveth and abideth forever.

James 1, 18. Of his own will begat he us with the word of truth.

1 John 3, 9. Whosoever is born of God, doth not commit sin; for his seed remaineth in him: and he cannot sin, because he is born of God.

1 John 5, 4. Whatsoever is born of God, overcometh the world.

10. *What do you mean by regeneration?*

That act of the Holy Ghost, by which we become partakers of the divine life, or new creatures in Christ Jesus.

* 2 Cor. 5, 17. If any man be in Christ, he is a new creature: old things are passed away, behold all things are become new.

Eph. 4, 24. Put on the new man, which after God is created in righteousness and true holiness.

Rom. 6, 4–6; Col. 3, 10; Gal. 3, 27 (put on Christ); 6, 15 (a new creature).

11. *Why do all men need regeneration?*

Because they are all born of the flesh, are dead in sin, and thus disqualified by nature for communion with a holy God.

* John 3, 6. That which is born of the flesh, is flesh; and that which is born of the Spirit, is spirit.

Eph. 2, 1. And you hath he quickened, who were dead in trespasses and sins.

Comp. Lessons XIX.–XXI.

12. *What are the effects of regeneration?*

By regeneration we become children of God, and heirs of eternal life.

John 1, 12. 13. As many as received him, to them gave he power to become the sons of God, even to them that believe on his name: which were born . . . of God.

* Rom. 8, 15–17. Ye have received the Spirit of adoption, whereby we cry, Abba, Father. The Spirit itself beareth witness with our spirit, that we are the children of God: and if children, then heirs; heirs of God, and joint heirs with Christ.

Gal. 4, 5. 6; Eph. 1, 5; 1 John 3, 1.

NOTES AND HINTS.

Q. 2 and 3. The question of the origin of sin and the precise relation of God's absolute sovereignty to man's relative freedom and accountability, is one of the most difficult problems in philosophy and theology, which will perhaps never be fully solved in the present imperfect state of human knowledge. God's sovereignty and man's freedom are like two arches which undoubtedly meet, although we may not see the connection. All true Christians may practically agree in ascribing their salvation to free grace without any merit of their own, and in tracing the condemnation of the wicked to their own guilt and unbelief. We must pray as if everything depended on God, and we must work as if everything depended on us. Paul puts both boldly together, Phil. 2:12, 13, and makes the former the reason and stimulus for the latter. What lies beyond is a matter of theological speculation, but not of public doctrine.

Q. 4. *Illumination* is frequently distinguished from vocation as a separate act of grace. But it may be more properly considered as the effectual calling in its operation upon the *mind*, or the act of the Holy Spirit, by which the eyes of our understanding are opened concerning our sin and misery and the salvation of Christ. Comp. John 16, 8-11; Acts 16, 18: 1 Cor. 2, 13; 2 Cor. 4, 6; Eph. 1, 17; Col. 1, 9. The *inspiration* of the apostles differs from the general *illumination* of all believers, not only as the highest degree of illumination, but also by its infallibility, or freedom from error in matters of faith.

Q. 5. The Greek term *metanoia*, which is uniformly translated *repentance* in the English Bible, signifies properly a *change of mind* or *of heart*, and corresponds to what we generally mean by *conversion*. It includes both *repentance*, *i.e.* the negative act of turning away from sin, and *faith*, *i.e.* the positive act of turning to God. Repentance and faith, though distinct, can never be separated in experience. True repentance is impossible without faith; and *vice versa*. We may, however, distinguish two kinds of repentance: (1) *legalistic* repentance, or the knowledge and hatred of sin awakened by the law of God as a schoolmaster to bring us to Christ, which precedes faith, and (2) *evangelical* repentance, which proceeds from the contemplation of the cross of Christ, and presupposes faith. Both act and react upon each other.

Q. 10. *Regeneration*, or the *new birth, heavenly birth*, as distinct from natural generation or earthly birth, is not merely a reformation or change of views and conduct, but a new moral creation, the implanting of the life of Christ in the soul by the Holy Spirit. This life is at first weak and tender, and needs the nursing care of the Church through the means of grace, that it may grow gradually to full maturity in Christ, and transform the mind, heart, and will into his holy image. Regeneration and conversion, though closely related, and inseparable in experience, differ in this,—that the former is the *divine* act, conversion the *human* act, in the same great moral change. In the one, man is passive (as in natural birth), in the other he is active. Yet no man can be converted without the enabling and renewing influence of the Holy Spirit, which must precede all the action of man. "Turn [convert] thou me, and I shall be turned," Jer. 31, 18. No one can come to Christ, except the Father draw him, John 6, 44. Regeneration, like natural birth, takes place but once, and, like baptism (with which it is closely connected in John 3, 5; Tit. 3, 5), cannot be repeated. But we may speak of a daily renewal of repentance and faith, or conversion, especially after a relapse, as in the cases of David, and Peter. Both terms, however, are sometimes used in a wider, sometimes in a narrower, sense.

Q. 12. The state of *adoption* (or "sonship" in Greek) is opposed to the state of bondage, and implies all the freedom and privileges of children and heirs in the house of their father. To be a child of God, the Maker of heaven and earth, the Giver of every good gift, is the highest honor and greatest wealth that can be imagined.

XXXIX. Justification and Sanctification.

1. *What is justification?*

Justification is an act of God, by which he pardons our sins, and applies to us the righteousness of Christ.

* Rom. 4, 7. 8 (comp. Ps. 32, 1. 2). Blessed are they whose iniquities are forgiven, and whose sins are covered. Blessed is the man to whom the Lord will not impute sin.

Isa. 1, 18. Though your sins be as scarlet, they shall be as white as snow; though they be red like crimson, they shall be as wool.

2 Cor. 5, 19. 21. God was in Christ, reconciling the world unto himself, not imputing their trespasses unto them ... He hath made him to be sin for us, who knew no sin; that we might be made the righteousness of God in him.

Rom. 10, 4. Christ is the end of the law for righteousness to every one that believeth.

Comp. Ps. 103, 3 (who forgiveth all thine iniquity, who healeth all thy diseases); Isa. 55, 7 (God will abundantly pardon); Jer. 31, 34 (I will forgive their iniquity, and remember their sin no more); Matt. 26, 28 (my blood which is shed for many for the remission of sins); Eph. 1, 7 (in whom we have redemption through his blood, the forgiveness of sins); Col. 1, 14; Acts 5, 31; 1 John 1, 7-9 (the blood of Jesus Christ cleanseth us from all sin); Heb. 9, 14; 1 Pet. 1, 19; Rev. 1, 5;—Rom. 1, 17 (the righteousness of God from faith to faith); 3, 21. 22; 4, 3-8; 5, 19 (by the obedience of one shall many be made righteous); 8, 30; 1 Cor. 1, 30 (Christ is made unto us ... righteousness).

2. *How is the sinner justified?*

By the free grace of God in Christ through

faith, which so unites us to Christ that he lives in us and we in him.

* Eph. 2, 8. By grace are ye saved through faith; and that not of yourselves: it is the gift of God.
Rom. 1, 16. 17. I am not ashamed of the gospel of Christ: for it is the power of God unto salvation to every one that believeth; to the Jew first, and also to the Greek [the Gentile]. For therein is the righteousness of God revealed from faith to faith: as it is written [Hab. 2, 4]: "The just shall live by faith." [This is the theme or leading thought of the Epistle to the Romans.]
Rom. 3, 24. Being justified freely by his grace through the redemption that is in Christ Jesus.
Gal. 2, 20. I am crucified with Christ: nevertheless I live: yet not I, but Christ liveth in me: and the life which I now live in the flesh, I live by the faith of the Son of God.
John 3, 36; Luke 18, 13. 14; Rom. 3, 28 (justified by faith without the deeds of the law); Gal. 2, 16 (justified by the faith of Christ, and not by the works of the law); Phil. 3, 9 (not having mine own righteousness, which is of the law, but that which is through the faith of Christ, the righteousness which is of God by faith); 2 Tim. 1, 9; Tit. 3, 5; Acts 15, 11.

3. *What is the effect of justification upon the heart?*

Peace with God, which passes all understanding.

* Rom. 5, 1. Being justified by faith, we have peace with God through our Lord Jesus Christ.
Comp. Phil. 4, 7; Eph. 2, 14; Col. 1, 20; 3, 15; John 14, 27.

4. *What is the evidence of justification?*

Good works, or a holy life.

* Matt. 5, 16. Let your light so shine before men, that they may see your good works and glorify your Father which is in heaven.
James 2, 17. Faith without works is dead.—Comp. v. 14–26.
Gal. 5, 24. They that are Christ's have crucified the flesh with the affections and lusts.
Matt. 7, 16 (ye shall know them by their fruits); John 15, 4. 5; Gal. 2, 17. 20; Rom. 6, 2–18. 22; 1 Cor. 13, 2: Heb. 12, 14 (without holiness no man shall see the Lord); Eph. 4, 23. 24 (in righteousness and true holiness); Col. 1, 10. 11 (fruitful in every good work); 1 John 3, 9; 2 Pet. 3, 11 (in all holy conversation and godliness).

5. Can there be true faith without good works?

No: true faith works by love, purifies the heart, overcomes the world, and abounds in fruits of righteousness.

Gal. 5, 6. Faith which worketh by love.

1 John 3, 3. Every man that has this hope in him purifieth himself, even as he is pure.

* 1 John 5, 4. Whatsoever is born of God overcometh the world: and this is the victory over the world, even our faith.

Comp. the passages in Question 4, and Lesson XII.

6. What is sanctification?

Sanctification is continual growth in grace through the indwelling power of the Holy Spirit upon our hearts, until we attain to perfection in Christ.

* 2 Pet. 3, 18. Grow in grace, and in the knowledge of our Lord and Saviour Jesus Christ.

* Matt. 5, 48. Be ye perfect, even as your Father which is in heaven is perfect.

1 Thess. 4, 3. This is the will of God, even your sanctification.

Rom. 6, 14. Sin shall not have dominion over you: for ye are not under the law, but under grace.

2 Cor. 7, 1. Having these promises, dearly beloved, let us cleanse ourselves from all filthiness of the flesh and spirit, perfecting holiness in the fear of God.

Comp. John 17, 17 (Sanctify them through thy truth); Eph. 4, 15 (grow up into Christ in all things); 1 Pet. 2, 2 (that ye may grow by the sincere milk of the word); Rom. 6, 2 ff.; 1 Thess. 4, 7 (God hath called us unto holiness); 2 Thess. 2, 13 (through sanctification of the Spirit); Eph. 1, 4 (holy and without blame before him in love); 4, 13 (till we all come ... unto a perfect man, unto the measure of the stature of the fulness of Christ); Phil. 3, 12–14 (I press toward the mark for the prize of the high calling of God in Christ Jesus).

7. What are the chief Christian graces or virtues?

Faith, hope, and love.

* 1 Cor. 13, 13. Now abideth faith, hope, charity [love], these three; but the greatest of these is charity.

Gal. 5, 22. The fruit of the Spirit is love, joy, peace, long-suffering, gentleness, goodness, faith, meekness, temperance.

2 Pet. 1, 5–7. Add to your faith virtue; and to virtue knowledge; and to knowledge temperance; and to temperance patience; and to patience godliness; and to godliness brotherly kindness; and to brotherly kindness charity.

8. *What is glorification?*

The completion of the work of grace at the coming of Christ, when we shall share in his glory and enjoy him forever.

* Col. 3, 4. When Christ, who is our life, shall appear, then shall ye also appear with him in glory.

Rom. 8, 30. Whom he justified, them he also glorified.

Phil. 1, 6. He which hath begun a good work in you, will perform it until the day of Jesus Christ.

1 John 3, 2. Beloved, now are we the sons of God, and it doth not yet appear what we shall be: but we know that, when he shall appear, we shall be like him; for we shall see him as he is.

Comp. John 17, 24 (that they may behold my glory); Rom. 5, 2 (we rejoice in hope of the glory of God); 1 Thess. 2, 12 (called unto his kingdom and glory); 2 Thess. 2, 14 (to the obtaining of the glory of our Lord Jesus Christ); 1 Pet. 5, 10 (called unto his eternal glory by Christ Jesus); 2 Cor. 3, 18 (from glory to glory).

Notes and Hints.

Q. 1 and 2. Justification is a judicial act of God, by which he places the sinner in right relation to himself; regeneration is an inward operation of the Holy Spirit, by which the sinner is transformed, or created anew in Christ. The former presupposes the latter, although in experience they cannot be separated.

The doctrine of justification by free grace through a living faith in Christ is a fundamental article of Protestantism as distinct from Romanism, and was more strongly urged by the Reformers than any other, except the doctrine of the absolute supremacy of the Scriptures in matters of faith. Romanism makes the Bible *and tradition co-ordinate* sources and rules of faith, and makes faith *and good works co-ordinate* conditions of justification; while Protestantism *subordinates* tradition to the Bible, and good works to faith, and measures their value by their agreement with the Bible and with faith.

Q. 2. The grace of God is the efficient primary *cause* of justification, the merits of Christ the procuring *cause* or (objective) *ground;* faith is the (subjective) *condition* on the part of man, or the instrument and organ of its appropriation. Justifying faith is not only a knowledge of the grace of God in Christ, but also a hearty confidence in the same, and a living union of the soul with Christ, so that we become partakers of his merits and all his benefits.

5. Good works are just as necessary and indispensable in the evangelical as they are in the Roman creed, only not as *conditions*, but as practical *fruits* or *evidences*, of justification. On this ground the apparent contradiction of St. Paul and St. James can be easily harmonized.

XL. The Resurrection of the Body, and the Life Everlasting.

1. *When will the work of grace be completed?*

At the glorious coming of our Lord Jesus Christ.

1 Thess. 5, 23. The very God of peace sanctify you wholly; and I pray God your whole spirit and soul and body be preserved blameless unto the coming of our Lord Jesus Christ.

1 Cor. 1, 7. 8; Col. 3, 4; Phil. 1, 6; 1 Pet. 1, 7–9; 2 Pet. 3, 12–14.

2. *What will take place at the coming of Christ?*

The resurrection of the dead, and the judgment of the world.

Compare, on the coming of Christ and the general judgment, Lesson XXXI.

3. *Shall all men rise again?*

Yes: the righteous shall rise unto the resurrection of life, the wicked unto the resurrection of damnation.

* John 5, 28. 29. The hour is coming, in the which all that are in the graves shall hear his voice, and shall come forth: they that have done good, unto the resurrection of life; and they that have done evil, unto the resurrection of damnation.

Dan. 12, 2. Many of them that sleep in the dust of the earth shall awake, some to everlasting life, and some to shame and everlasting contempt.

Matt. 25, 46. And these shall go away into everlasting punishment: but the righteous into life eternal.

Acts 24, 15. There shall be a resurrection of the dead, both of the just and unjust.

4. *How will the resurrection be effected?*

By the almighty power of God, who first

made man of the dust, and can also raise him from the dust.

Matt. 19, 26. With God all things are possible.—Comp. Gen. 2, 7; Phil. 3, 21.

John 12, 24. Except a corn of wheat fall into the ground and die, it abideth alone: but if it die, it bringeth forth much fruit.

1 Cor. 15, 35. 36. But some man will say: How are the dead raised up? and with what body do they come? Thou fool, that which thou sowest is not quickened, except it die.

5. *Where is the soul of the believer between death and the resurrection?*

In blessed communion with Christ, waiting for the glorious resurrection of the body, and for the consummation of the kingdom of God.

* Luke 23, 43. Jesus said unto him [the penitent thief]: Verily I say unto thee: To-day shalt thou be with me in paradise.

John 14, 2. In my Father's house are many mansions. ... I go to prepare a place for you.

Phil. 1, 23. I am in a strait betwixt two, having a desire to depart, and to be with Christ; which is far better.

2 Cor. 5, 1. 2. 8; 1 Thess. 4, 17; 2 Tim. 4, 6–8.

6. *On what ground do you rest your hope of a blessed resurrection?*

On the resurrection of Christ, and our living union with him.

* John 14, 19. Because I live, ye shall live also.

John 11, 25. I am the resurrection, and the life: he that believeth in me, though he were dead, yet shall he live.

1 Cor. 15, 20. Christ is risen from the dead, and become the first fruits of them that slept.

Job 19, 25. I know that my Redeemer liveth.

Rom. 8, 11; 1 Cor. 15, 12–23; Col. 1, 18 (the first born from the dead); Rev. 1, 5.

7. *What will be the nature of the resurrection-body of believers?*

It will be a spiritual body, immortal, incorruptible, and like unto the glorious body of Jesus Christ.

* Phil. 3, 20. 21. Our conversation is in heaven; from whence we also look for the Saviour, the Lord Jesus Christ: who shall change our vile body, that it may be fashioned like unto his glorious body.
1 Cor. 15, 42–44. It is sown in corruption; it is raised in incorruption: it is sown in dishonor; it is raised in glory: it is sown in weakness; it is raised in power: it is sown a natural body: it is raised a spiritual body. There is a natural body, and there is a spiritual body.
Dan. 12, 3. They that be wise shall shine as the brightness of the firmament; and they that turn many to righteousness, as the stars for ever and ever.

The resurrection body of the wicked, on the contrary, shall be "an abhorring unto all flesh" (Isa. 66, 24; Dan. 12, 2), and complete their misery.

8. *What will follow the resurrection of believers?*

The life everlasting, which begins already here with faith in Christ, but which will then be gloriously perfected.

* John, 6, 47. He that believeth on me hath everlasting life.
Ps. 16, 11. Thou wilt show me the path of life: in thy presence is fulness of joy; at thy right hand there are pleasures for evermore.
1 John 3, 2. Beloved, now are we the sons of God, and it doth not yet appear what we shall be: but we know that, when he shall appear, we shall be like him; for we shall see him as he is.
John 3, 15. 16. 36; 6, 40; Rom. 8, 17. 18. 23. 24; 2 Tim. 4, 8.

9. *What do you mean by the life everlasting in heaven?*

A state of perfect freedom from sin and death, and of unspeakable joy and glory in unbroken communion with the triune God and the innumerable company of saints and angels.

* 1 Cor. 2, 9. Eye hath not seen, nor ear heard, neither have entered the heart of man, the things which God hath prepared for them that love him.—Comp. Isa. 64, 4.

John 14, 2. 3. In my Father's house are many mansions.... [g] to prepare a place for you.... I will receive you unto myself; that where I am, there ye may be also.

Rev. 21, 4. God shall wipe away all tears from their eyes; and there shall be no more death, neither sorrow, nor crying, neither shall there be any more pain.

Compare John 17, 24 (that they may behold my glory); Matt. 25, 23 (enter into the joy of thy Lord); Luke 20, 36 (neither can they die any more; for they are equal unto the angels); 1 Cor. 15, 54 (death is swallowed up in victory); 1 Cor. 13, 8 (love never faileth); Heb. 4, 9 (a rest to the people of God); Rev. 14, 13 (they rest from their labors); Rom. 8, 21 (the glorious liberty of the children of God); 1 Pet. 1, 4 (an inheritance incorruptible, and undefiled, and that fadeth not away, reserved in heaven for you); v. 8 (rejoice with joy unspeakable and full of glory); 2 Pet. 3, 13 (new heavens and a new earth, wherein dwelleth righteousness); 1 Thess. 4, 17 (and so shall we ever be with the Lord); Heb. 12, 22. 23 (the heavenly Jerusalem, an innumerable company of angels, the general assembly and church of the firstborn); 2 Tim. 2, 12 (reign with Christ); Rev. 3, 21 (sit with me in my throne); 7, 14–17; 21, 1–7; 22, 1–5.

10. *What are the employments of the saints in heaven?*

They will see God, and love, serve, and praise him forever.

* Matt. 5, 8. Blessed are the pure in heart: for they shall see God.

1 Cor. 13, 12. Now we see through a glass, darkly; but then face to face: now I know in part; but then shall I know even as also I am known.

Rev. 7, 15. They are before the throne of God, and serve him day and night in his temple.

Rev. 5, 11. 12. I heard the voice of many angels round about the throne, and the beasts, and the elders: and the number of them was ten thousand times ten thousand, and thousands of thousands; saying with a loud voice: Worthy is the Lamb that was slain to receive power, and riches, and wisdom, and strength, and honor, and glory, and blessing.

Compare 1 John 3, 2 (we shall see him as he is); Rev. 22, 4 (they shall see his face); Ps. 145, 2 (I will praise thy name for ever and ever), and other Psalms of thanksgiving and praise; Rev. 4, 9–11; 5, 9–14 (they sung a new song, saying: Thou art worthy, etc.).

11. *What effect should this hope have upon you?*

It should inspire me to lead a holy life in the fear and love of God, so that I may die in peace and attain at last to the glorious resurrection of the just.

* 1 Cor. 15, 58. Therefore, my beloved brethren, be ye steadfast, unmovable, always abounding in the work of the Lord, forasmuch as ye know that your labor is not in vain in the Lord.

2 Pet. 3, 14. Wherefore, beloved, seeing that ye look for such things [for new heavens and a new earth, v. 13], be diligent that ye may be found of him in peace, without spot and blameless.

1 Tim. 4, 8. Godliness is profitable unto all things, having promise of the life that now is, and of that which is to come.

1 Thess. 3, 13; 5, 23; Phil. 1, 10; 2 Pet. 3, 11.

PART THIRD.

The Christian Life.

XLI. The Ten Commandments.

1 *What is your duty in view of what God has done for you?*

To be thankful for so great a salvation from sin and death, and to present myself a living sacrifice unto God.

* Rom. 12, 1. I beseech you therefore, brethren, by the mercies of God, that ye present your bodies a living sacrifice, holy, acceptable unto God, which is your reasonable service.

1 Cor. 6, 20. Ye are bought with a price: therefore glorify God in your body, and in your spirit, which are God's.

2 Cor. 5, 14. 15. The love of Christ constraineth us. ... He died for all, that they which live should not henceforth live unto themselves, but unto him which died for them, and rose again.

1 John 4, 19. We love him [or, rather: Let us love him, viz., God], because he first loved us.—Comp. v. 7 and 11.

Col. 1, 12–14; 1 Pet. 2, 9.

2. *How do you prove your thankfulness to God?*

By keeping God's holy law.

* Eccl. 12, 13. Fear God, and keep his commandments: for this is the whole duty of man.

* John 14, 15. If ye love me, keep my commandments.

1 John 5, 3. This is the love of God, that we keep his commandments: and his commandments are not grievous [burdensome, comp. Matt 11, 30].

Comp. John 14, 21. 23; 15, 10. 14; 1 John 2, 5.

3. What is the substance of the law of God?

Love to God, and love to our neighbor.

* Matt. 22, 37–40. Thou shalt love the Lord thy God with all thy heart, and with all thy soul, and with all thy mind. This is the first and great commandment. And the second is like unto it: Thou shalt love thy neighbor as thyself. On these two commandments hang all the law and the prophets.
Rom. 13, 10. Love is the fulfilling of the law.
Deut. 6, 5; 10, 12; Lev. 19, 18; John 13, 34. 35; Rom. 12, 10; 1 Cor. 13, 1–13; Gal. 5, 14; Eph. 5, 2; 1 Pet. 4, 8; 1 John 2, 9. 10; 3, 10. 11. 14–19; 4, 7. 8. 11. 16–21; James 2, 8.

4. Where is the moral law briefly summed up?

In the decalogue, or the ten commandments, which God gave through Moses to the people of Israel from Mount Sinai, after their deliverance from Egypt, and before their entrance into the land of promise.

Ex. 20, 1–10. Comp. Deut. 5, 1–22.

5. What is the use and design of the law?

It is to all men a mirror of the holy will of God, and of their own sinfulness; to the unconverted, a wholesome restraint, and schoolmaster to bring them unto Christ; to the converted, a rule of holy living.

Rom. 3, 20. By the law is the knowledge of sin.—Comp. 7, 7.
Gal. 3, 24. The law was our schoolmaster to bring us unto Christ.
Luke 16, 17. It is easier for heaven and earth to pass, than one tittle of the law to fail.
Comp. Matt. 5, 18. 19; 22, 37–40; Rom. 3, 31; 1 Cor. 6, 9. 10; Eph. 5, 5.

6. But has Christ not abolished the law?

No: he has fulfilled the law in his doctrine and life; he has redeemed us from its curse; and he enables us, by his Holy Spirit, to keep it in its true spiritual sense.

* Matt. 5, 17. Think not that I am come to destroy the law, or the prophets: I am not come to destroy, but to fulfil.

Gal. 3, 13. Christ hath redeemed us from the curse of the law.

Rom. 7, 22. I delight in the law of God after the inward man.

Comp. the whole Sermon on the Mount, Matt. 5–7, which is the evangelical legislation from the mount of beatitudes, and explains the deeper spiritual sense of the law

7. *How are the ten commandments divided?*

Into two tables, each consisting of five commandments.*

Ex. 31, 18. God gave unto Moses ... two tables of testimony, tables of stone, written with the finger of God.

Deut. 4, 13; 5, 22. Comp. 2 Cor. 3, 3.

8. *Of what does the first table treat?*

Of our duties to God, or of love to God.

Matt. 22, 37. 38. Thou shalt love the Lord thy God with all thy heart, and with all thy soul, and with all thy mind. This is the first and great commandment.

Mark 12, 30; Luke 10, 27; Deut. 6, 5; 10, 12; 30, 16. 12.

9. *Of what does the second table treat?*

Of our duties to man, or of love to our neighbor.

Matt. 22, 39. And the second is like unto it: Thou shalt love thy neighbor as thyself.

Mark 12, 31; Luke 10, 27; Rom. 13, 9; Lev. 19, 18.

10. *What does each commandment comprehend?*

Each commandment enjoins a virtue, and forbids the opposite sin.

NOTES AND HINTS.

Q. 4. The ten commandments are called the *moral* law, as distinct from the *civil* and *ceremonial* law, and are binding on all men and all times; while the ceremonial law was national and temporary in its character, with a typical reference to Christ. Hence the extraordinary solemnity with which the decalogue was promulgated directly by God under the manifestation of his holy majesty (Ex. 19), and recorded by his own finger on two tables of stone. It was, moreover, preserved in the ark of the covenant, in the holy of holies of the tabernacle, and the

* See notes pp. 138, 149.

temple, as the immovable foundation of the divine government and of all social order and well-being. The number *ten* symbolizes the comprehensiveness and completeness of this moral law. The civil and ceremonial law of the Jewish theocracy rested on the decalogue, and, according to more recent research (Bertheau and others), is divided into seven groups, each with ten commandments.

Q. 5. The Lutheran Catechisms treat of the ten commandments before the Creed, because they view the law mainly in its Old Testament aspect, as a schoolmaster, and a mirror of sin. The Reformed Catechisms (Calvin's, or the Genevan, the Heidelberg, the Anglican, the Westminster), regarding the law in its New Testament sense, as the rule of Christian life, place the commandments after the Creed, since it is only by true faith in Christ and the power of his Holy Spirit that we are enabled to keep the law of God and to practise, Christian virtues. But in the explanation of the commandments, with the exception of the second and the fourth, all these Catechisms essentially agree.

Q. 7. As the Bible does not define the number of commandments on each table, there is room for difference of opinion: the Lutheran Catechisms (which omit the second commandment altogether) assign three to the first and seven to the second table: the Reformed Catechisms, four to the first and six to the second table. We make an equal division of five for each table: see note to Lesson XLVI. Q. 1. The difference, however, is more a matter of form.

The tables of stone symbolize the inviolability and unchangeableness of the divine law.

Q. 10. Thus, the first commandment forbids idolatry, and enjoins the worship of one God; the third prohibits the abuse, and commands the right use, of the name of God; the fourth enjoins the sanctification, and forbids the desecration, of the sabbath; the fifth commands respect, love, and obedience to parental authority, and prohibits disrespect and disobedience; the seventh prohibits adultery and all sexual impurity, and enjoins chastity; the eighth forbids stealing, and enjoins honesty and labor (comp. Eph. 4, 28: "Let him that stole steal no more, but rather let him labor," etc.) In the Old Testament, especially in the second table, the negative prohibitions preponderate, for the reason that the ten commandments had a civil and political as well as religious and ecclesiastical significance, and are to this day the foundation of all good government, which can and must prohibit and punish vice, but cannot command and enforce positive virtue. But the Christian Church explains the law in the light of the gospel, and of the example of Christ, who is the perfect model of every virtue.

XLII. The First Commandment.

1. *What is the preface to the ten commandments?*

I am the Lord thy God, who have brought thee out of the land of Egypt, out of the house of bondage.

Ex. 20, 2. Deut. 5, 6.

THE FIRST COMMANDMENT.

2. *What does this mean?*

God reminds us thereby of his holy majesty, and of his redeeming mercy, that we may keep his law not only from fear, but from gratitude and love.

Lev. 18, 30; 19, 37; 1 Pet. 1, 15–19; 2 Cor. 5, 14. 15.

3. *What is the first commandment?*

Thou shalt have no other gods before Me.

Ex. 20, 3.   Deut. 5, 7.

4. *What does God forbid in this commandment?*

All kinds of idolatry, or creature-worship.

1 John 5, 21.   Keep yourselves from idols.
1 Cor. 10, 14.   Flee from idolatry.

5. *What is idolatry?*

The worship of any thing which is not God, as the stars, or animals, or men, or angels, or human imaginations.

Gal. 4, 8. When ye knew not God, ye did service unto them which by nature are no gods.

Comp. Rom. 1, 21–32, on the origin and progress of idolatry and its immoral consequences.

Examples: The *golden calf* (probably in remembrance of the Egyptian worship of the ox), Ex. 32, 4 ff.; *Baal* (the god of the sun), often worshipped by the Jews in the period of the judges, and the later kings, especially Ahab and Manasseh, 2 Chron. 28, 2; 2 Kings 21, 3, etc.; *Moloch* (likewise a form of star-worship, connected with sacrifices of children), Lev. 18, 21; 2 Kings 16, 3, etc.; *the brazen serpent*, originally erected as a symbol and type of redemption, Numb. 21, 9 (comp. John 3, 14), but afterwards divinely worshipped, 2 Kings 18, 6; the worship of *men*, Acts 10, 25. 26; Rev. 19, 10; of *angels*, Col. 2, 18.—The ancient Greek and Roman idolatry consisted in the worship of great men and women, or the powers of nature, or mere creations of fancy. The gross form of idolatry still prevails among the many millions of heathen.

THE FIRST COMMANDMENT. 135

6. *What else may be called idolatry?*

All improper attachment to ourselves, to the world, or to any creature, whereby we detract from the supreme honor and love due to God.

Examples of the refined forms of idolatry which still continue even among Christians: excessive love of *riches*, Matt. 6, 24 (Ye cannot serve God and mammon); 1 Tim. 6, 17; Eph. 5, 5; Col. 3, 5 (covetousness, which is *idolatry*); Job 31, 24; *sensual enjoyment*, Rom. 16, 18; Phil. 3, 19 (whose end is destruction, whose god is their belly); *father* or *mother*, *son* or *daughter*, if preferred to Christ, Matt. 10, 37; Luke 14, 26; *man*, Acts 10, 25. 26; Rev. 19, 10; Jer. 17, 5; the *world* generally, 1 John 2, 15–17 (Love not the world, neither the things that are in the world).

7. *What does God require in this commandment?*

That we fear and love God above all things, worship him only, put all our trust in him, and find our highest joy and delight in him.

* Matt. 4, 10. Thou shalt worship the Lord thy God, and him only shalt thou serve.

Ps. 111, 10. The fear of the Lord is the beginning of wisdom.

Prov. 23, 26. My son, give me thine heart.

Ps. 73, 25. 26. Whom have I in heaven but thee? and there is none upon earth that I desire beside thee. My flesh and my heart faileth: but God is the strength of my heart, and my portion forever.

Matt. 22, 37; John 4, 23. 24; 1 Thess. 1, 9 (Ye turned to God from idols to serve the true and living God); Ps. 18, 1. 2; 29, 2; 32, 11; 37, 4.

NOTES AND HINTS.

Q. 1 and 2. Literal version: "I, Jehovah, am thy God," etc. The name *Jehovah* which occurs in the preface, also in the second, third, fourth, and fifth commandments, and is generally translated *Lord* (because the Jews, from reverence, never pronounced it, but *Adonai* = *Lord*, instead), is the specific name of the God of revelation, the God of his people (*thy* God), the faithful, unchangeable God of the covenant, who is true to all his promises: comp. Ex. 3, 14; 6, 2–4; Isa. 42, 8; Rev. 1, 4. *Elohim, God*, is the general name, the God of nature, the God of the Gentiles as well as the Jews, the almighty Maker of heaven and earth (hence it occurs exclusively in Gen. 1). The reference to the deliverance of Israel from the bondage of Egypt elicits gratitude and love as the proper motive and soul of obedience to God's commandments. In its Christian application, it reminds us of the far greater mercy of God in Christ, who delivered us from the slavery of sin and death, and thus has a still stronger claim upon our gratitude and obedience (1 John 4, 18. 19; 5, 3; 2 Cor. 5, 14. 15).

Q. 5. With the gross forms of idolatry are generally connected pernicious superstitions, as sorcery, magic, soothsaying, necromancy, witchcraft,—all of which are strictly forbidden in the law, Deut. 18, 10-12; Lev. 19, 31; Mic. 5, 12. To the same class belong the modern delusions of so-called spiritualism. Superstition is a relic of heathen idolatry. Infidelity often passes over into superstition. Man must believe in something, either in God or in idols, either in the Holy Ghost or in spectres, either in providence or a dark fate.

XLIII. The Second Commandment.

1. *What is the second commandment?*

Thou shalt not make unto thee any graven image, or any likeness *of any thing* that *is* in heaven above, or that *is* in the earth beneath, or that *is* in the water under the earth: thou shalt not bow down thyself to them, nor serve them.

For I the Lord thy God *am* a jealous God, visiting the iniquity of the fathers upon the children unto the third and fourth *generation* of them that hate Me; and shewing mercy unto thousands of them that love Me, and keep My commandments.

Ex. 20, 4-6.—Deut. 5, 7-10.

2. *What does God forbid in this commandment?*

The worship of images, and all false modes of worship which are contrary to the word of God.

Ps. 97, 7. Confounded be all they that serve graven images, that boast themselves of idols.

Rom. 1, 22. 23. Professing themselves to be wise, they [the heathen] became fools, and changed the glory of the uncorruptible God into an image made like to corruptible man, and to birds, and fourfooted beasts, and creeping things.

Acts 17, 29. We ought not to think that the Godhead is like unto gold, or silver, or stone, graven by art and man's device.

Ex. 23, 24 (Thou shalt not bow down to their gods); 34, 13. 14 (ye shall destroy their altars, break their statues, and cut

THE SECOND COMMANDMENT.

down their groves); Deut. 4, 23; 12, 3. 32; Judg. 2, 2; Isa. 40, 25 (To whom then will ye liken me, or shall I be equal?); Hab. 2, 18. 19 (What profiteth the graven image, ... the molten image, and a teacher of lies, that the maker of his work trusteth therein, to make dumb idols?).

3. Are all images, then, forbidden by God?

No: images of creatures are allowed, but not for idolatrous, or superstitious uses.

Ex. 35, 30–33. The Lord hath filled Bezaleel with the Spirit of God, in wisdom, in understanding, and in knowledge, and in all manner of workmanship; and to devise curious works, to work in gold, and in silver, and in brass, and in the cutting of stones, to set them, and in carving of wood, to make any manner of cunning work.

Comp. Ex. 31, 2–11; 1 Kings 7, 14. The *brazen serpent* was erected by divine command as a symbol of redemption, Numb. 21, 8, 9; comp. John 3, 14. 15. So also the *cherubim*, which overshadowed with their wings the ark of the covenant in the holy of holies, and symbolically represented the whole living creation, Ex. 25, 17 ff.; 37, 6 ff.; comp. Ez. 41, 18; Heb. 9, 5; Rev. 4, 6 ff., etc.

4. What does God enjoin in this commandment?

That we worship God, who is a Spirit, in spirit and in truth.

* John 4, 24. God is a Spirit: and they that worship him must worship him in spirit and in truth.

Ps. 29, 2. Give unto the Lord the glory due unto his name; worship the Lord in the beauty of holiness.

5. What belongs to the true worship of God?

The reading of the Holy Scriptures, the preaching of the gospel, prayer and praise, and the administration of the sacraments according to God's appointment.

(1.) Reading, hearing, and exposition of the word of God: Deut. 17, 18. 19; 31, 10–13; Neh. 8, 2–8;—Luke 4, 16; Acts 13, 15. 27; 15, 21; 17, 11; Col. 4, 16; 1 Thess. 5, 27; 2 Tim. 3, 16. 17; James 1, 22. 23; 2 Pet. 1, 19–21; Rev. 1, 3.

(2.) Preaching of the gospel: Matt. 4, 17; Mark 16, 15; Acts 5, 42; Rom. 10, 14. 15. 17; 1 Cor. 1, 21–24; 2 Tim. 4, 1 2; 1 Pet. 1, 25.

THE SECOND COMMANDMENT.

(3.) Prayer and praise (including singing): Ps. 95, 6. 7; Eph. 5, 19. 20 (psalms, and hymns, and spiritual songs, singing and making melody in your heart to the Lord); Col. 3, 16; Phil. 4, 6; 1 Tim. 2, 1. 2; Rev. 5, 13, and innumerable other passages.

(4.) Administration of the sacraments: Holy baptism, Matt. 28, 19, etc.; the Lord's Supper, Matt. 26, 26, etc.

6. *How does God enforce this commandment?*

By reminding us of his zeal for the purity of worship, by threatening us with his wrath, and promising his mercy unto children and children's children.

Deut. 5, 29. O that there were such a heart in them that they would fear me, and keep all my commandments always, that it might be well with them, and with their children forever!—1 Cor. 10, 20–22.

7. *Why does he thus enforce this commandment?*

Because God is unwilling to give his honor to any other, and because apostasy from the true worship of the Lord our God is the fruitful source of all manner of superstition and vice.

Isa. 42, 8. My glory will I not give to another, neither my praise to graven images.

Ps. 115, 1. Not unto us, O Lord, not unto us, but unto thy name give glory.

Comp. Rom. 1, 21–32, where the progress of idolatry and image-worship is traced to its practical consequences.

NOTES AND HINTS.

The Roman Catholic Church, following Augustine and Jerome in the fifth century, regards the second commandment only as an explanation of the first, and in her catechisms generally omits it altogether, but divides the tenth commandment into two, in order thus to restore the number ten. Hence the different modes of counting from the second to the ninth commandment; our third commandment being the second in the Roman Catholic Catechisms, and so on to the tenth. Luther, in his Catechism, retained this division, more from traditional habit than from principle. But the Catechisms of the Reformed Church both on the continent and in England and Scotland, following the example of the ancient Jews (see Josephus), the early Fathers, and the Greek Church, strictly adhere to the text in Ex. 20, without any omission, thus restoring the second commandment to its proper place, and leaving the tenth undivided. The second commandment, though closely related to the first, differs from it in prohibiting *image-worship* and enjoining the *true worship*, while the first prohibits *idolatry* and enjoins *monotheism*. The best modern divines, of the Lutheran Church, also justify the Reformed division, and a number of commentaries on

Luther's Smaller Catechism, accordingly, treat the ninth and tenth commandments as one.

Q. 1. The words: "that is in heaven above," refer to the worship of the sun, moon, and stars; the words: "in the earth beneath," to the worship of man and animals; the words: "in the water," to the worship of the crocodile;—all of which were objects of divine adoration with the Egyptians and other heathen nations.

Q. 2. The second commandment unquestionably prohibits the making and worshipping of all kinds of *idols*, whether they be of gold, silver, brass, wood, or color, whether works of sculpture or painting (comp. Ex. 20, 23; 34, 13. 14; Deut. 4, 15–18), as also all visible representations of the invisible Godhead, that dwells in light inaccessible, and cannot be likened to any creature (1 Tim. 6, 16; Deut. 4, 15–18; Isa. 40, 18. 25; 46, 5). Even Christ, who is the visible image of the invisible God, can not be represented according to his *divine* nature, although he may and has often been represented *symbolically* (in the figure of the good Shepherd, or the Lamb), and according to his *human* nature. The gospel history, no doubt for wise reasons, is completely silent on the personal appearance of the Saviour. Hence we have no reliable picture of him; and even the highest creations of a Raphael, Dürer, Correggio, Titian, are unsatisfactory, when they attempt to give visible shape and form to the absolute ideal of spotless purity and moral perfection.

Q. 3. The representation of *creatures* by works of art is not contrary to Scripture (see the passages quoted, Q. 3). All fine arts—architecture, painting, sculpture, music, and poetry—come from God, and should be consecrated to the service of religion, especially poetry and music. Their noblest mission is to elevate, adorn, and beautify the worship of Him who is the Author of all beauty, truth, and goodness. It is sometimes charged upon the Reformed Church that it was originally opposed to all pictures; but the charge is unjust. Calvin, in his Catechism, says expressly: "The second commandment is not to be understood as condemning the arts of painting and sculpture in general; but we are only forbidden to make images for the purpose of seeking or worshipping God in them, or to abuse them in any way for superstition and idolatry." Pictures for purposes of *instruction*, or *commemoration*, or *ornament*, are innocent, and useful, especially in the education of children. They are inseparably connected with the progress of civilization, and sanctioned by the history of Christian art from the earliest times to the present. But the abuse of pictures and statues, or any other works of art, in the service of superstition and idolatry, is a plain violation of the second commandment. Thus, it is still customary in the Roman Church—especially in those countries where it exclusively prevails—to pay divine honors to images of saints, and of the Virgin Mary, and to crucifixes, by kissing them, kneeling before them, offering them incense, sacrifices, and prayers, and ascribing to them miraculous cures. This superstitious and idolatrous practice, which commenced in the fourth century and became widely prevalent during the middle ages, although not without continued protest from the friends of a purer and more spiritual worship, was no doubt the chief, if not the only, cause of the omission of the second commandment, which so plainly condemns all idolatrous use of images. As there is a gross and a refined idolatry, so there is also a gross (heathen) and a refined (Roman Catholic) image worship.

Q. 6 and 7. It is to be observed that the punishment of God is threatened upon those that *hate* God, and his mercy promised to those that *love* him. Thus, the second commandment, like the first and the last, points to the *heart*, as the secret fountain of false or true worship, and of disobedience or obedience to the whole law of God.—Comp. Deut. 6, 5 (with all thy *heart*); Matt. 22 40.

XLIV. The Third Commandment.

1. *What is the third commandment?*

Thou shalt not take the name of the Lord thy God in vain.

For the Lord will not hold him guiltless that taketh His name in vain.

Ex. 20, 7.—Deut. 5, 11.

2. *What do you understand by the name of God?*

Every thing by which God makes himself known to us,—his names, titles, attributes, words, works, and ordinances.

3. *What does God forbid in this commandment?*

False and rash oaths, blasphemy, cursing, swearing, and all profanity in thought and speech.

* Matt. 5, 34–37. Swear not at all: neither by heaven; for it is God's throne: nor by the earth; for it is his footstool: neither by Jerusalem; for it is the city of the great King. Neither shalt thou swear by thy head, because thou canst not make one hair white or black. But let your communication be, Yea, yea; Nay, nay: for whatsoever is more than these cometh of evil.

Rom. 12, 14. Bless, and curse not.

Lev. 19, 12; 24, 14–16; Matt. 23, 21. 22; James 5, 12.

4. *In what cases are Christians allowed to swear?*

When the magistrate, as the minister of God, demands an oath or affirmation for the maintenance of truth and justice.

Ex. 22, 11 (Then shall an oath of the Lord be between them both); Deut. 6, 13; 10, 20 (Thou shalt fear the Lord thy God. ... and swear by his name); Josh. 9, 15. 19; Isa. 45, 23 (I have sworn by myself); 65, 16; Matt. 26, 63. 64 (Christ before the highpriest): Heb. 6, 13 (God sware by himself; ... confirmed it by an oath; comp. Gen. 22, 16).

THE THIRD COMMANDMENT.

5. *What is required in the third commandment?*

That we think and speak with deep reverence of God and all holy things, and glorify the name of the Lord in our lives.

1 Chron. 16, 29. Worship the Lord in the beauty of holiness.
* 1 Cor. 10, 31. Whatsoever ye do, do all to the glory of God.
Ps. 95, 6; 103, 1–4; Rom. 9, 5 (God blessed forever) 2 Cor. 11, 31 (blessed for evermore); Gal. 1, 5 (to whom be glory for ever and ever); Eph. 5, 19, 20; 1 Pet. 4, 11 (that God in all things may be glorified through Jesus Christ); 1 Cor. 6, 20; Rev. 15, 3. 4.

6. *Why is a special warning added to this commandment?*

Because sins of profanity are often overlooked or slightly thought of by men, but are, nevertheless, an abomination before God, and expose us to his righteous judgment.

Zech. 5, 3. Every one that sweareth shall be cut off.
Comp. Levit. 24, 10–16 (He that blasphemeth the name of the Lord, he shall surely be put to death, and all the congregation shall certainly stone him); Malachi 3, 5; Gal. 6, 7 (Be not deceived; God is not mocked); Heb. 10, 31 (It is a fearful thing to fall into the hands of the living God).

NOTES AND HINTS.

Q. 2. Hence it is equally sinful to swear by the name of Jesus, or by the Holy Ghost, or by the Eternal, or by the Bible, or by the sacrament, or by heaven, etc.—Comp. Matt. 23, 21. 22.

Q. 3. There are different kinds of rash and useless swearing, with corresponding degrees of guilt; arising, (1) from ignorance or thoughtlessness; (2) from superstition; (3) from bad habit; (4) from malice and wickedness.

Q. 4. A public oath before the magistrate is a solemn appeal to God as witness to the truth, for the public good, and may be regarded as an act of worship, by which we acknowledge God as the searcher of hearts and avenger of all falsehood and perjury. Such oaths cannot be safely dispensed with in a sinful, lying world. In the perfect kingdom of God there will be no more falsehood and distrust, consequently no necessity for oaths. This end should be continually kept in view, so that the word of Christ, Matt. 5, 33–37, may be more and more fulfilled in its strict sense. The conscientious scruples of Quakers and Mennonites against all oaths arise from a literal interpretation of Matt. 5. 33–37 and James 5, 12, without proper regard to the other passages on the subject (see Q. 4), and to the distinction between the present and 33–37 and James 5, 12. In the United States they are allowed simply to *affirm*, instead of swearing.

XLV. The Fourth Commandment.

1. *What is the fourth commandment?*

Remember the sabbath day, to keep it holy. Six days shalt thou labor, and do all thy work: but the seventh day *is* the sabbath of the Lord thy God: *in it* thou shalt not do any work, thou, nor thy son, nor thy daughter, thy manservant, nor thy maidservant, nor thy cattle, nor thy stranger that *is* within thy gates.

For *in* six days the Lord made heaven and earth, the sea, and all that in them *is*, and rested the seventh day: wherefore the Lord blessed the sabbath day, and hallowed it.

Ex. 20, 8-11.—Deut. 5, 12-15.

2. *What does God forbid in this commandment?*

All desecration of the day of holy rest, either by secular labor and amusement, or by idleness and neglect of divine worship.

Levit. 23, 3. Six days shall work be done: but the seventh day is the sabbath of rest, a holy convocation; ye shall do no work therein: it is the sabbath of the Lord in all your dwellings.

Comp. Lev. 31, 13-17; Isa. 56, 2; 58, 13; Jer. 17, 21. 22: Neh. 13, 16-19; Matt. 24, 20; Luke 23, 56 (They rested the sabbath day according to the commandment).

3. *Are all works, then, prohibited on the Lord's Day?*

No: acts of worship, charity, and necessity are allowed, and commended by the example of our Saviour.

The Saviour performed many miracles of mercy on the sabbath-day, as the healing of the infirm woman, Luke 13, 11-16, the woman with the dropsy, 14, 2-5, the sick man with a withered hand, Matt. 12, 10–13, the diseased at the pool of Bethesda, John 5, 16, and the blind man, 9, 14. The Saviour, moreover, ate, and justified the preparation of food on the sabbath, Luke 14, 1; Matt. 12, 1–5; as also the saving of a sheep, Matt. 12, 11. 12, and the watering of an ox or an ass, Luke 13, 15. All works connected with public worship and pastoral care are likewise proper works for the sabbath. Comp. James 2, 27, " Pure religion and undefiled before God and the Father is this, to visit the fatherless and widows in their affliction, and to keep himself unspotted from the world."

4. *How is the Lord's Day to be kept holy?*

By acts of public and private worship, by devotional reading and meditation, by godly conversation and works of Christian charity.

* Col. 3, 16. Let the word of God dwell in you richly in all wisdom, teaching and admonishing one another in psalms and hymns and spiritual songs, singing with grace in your hearts to the Lord.

Lev. 19, 30. Ye shall keep my sabbaths, and reverence my sanctuary: I am the Lord.

Ezek. 20, 12. I gave them my sabbaths, to be a sign between me and them, that they might know that I am the Lord that sanctify them.

Luke 4, 16. Jesus came to Nazareth, where he had been brought up: and, as his custom was, he went into the synagogue on the sabbath day, and stood up for to read [the Scriptures].

Ps. 118, 24. This is the day which the Lord hath made; we will rejoice and be glad in it.

Comp. Ex. 31, 16. 17; Isa. 58, 13 (Call the sabbath a delight, the holy of the Lord, honorable, etc.); 66, 23 (from one sabbath to another ... to worship before me); Acts 13, 14 (Paul and Barnabas went into the synagogue on the sabbath day); 15, 21 (Moses ... being read in the synagogues every sabbath day); 16, 13; 17, 2 (Paul reasoned with them three sabbath days out of the Scriptures).

Comp. on the proper observance of the Christian sabbath, Acts 20, 7; 1 Cor. 16, 2; Rev. 1, 10; also Col. 3, 16; Eph. 5, 19. 20; 1 Cor. 14, 26; Heb. 10, 25.

5. *Why was the Jewish sabbath celebrated on the seventh day of the week?*

To commemorate the creation, and the redemption of Israel from the bondage of Egypt.

Gen. 2, 2. 3; Ex. 20, 11; Deut. 5, 15.

6. *Why is the Christian sabbath celebrated on the first day of the week?*

To commemorate the resurrection of Christ, and our redemption from the bondage of sin and death, for which reason it is also called "the Lord's Day."

Acts 20, 7. And upon the first day of the week, when the disciples came together to break bread, Paul preached unto them, ready to depart on the morrow; and continued his speech until midnight.

1 Cor. 16, 2. Upon the first day of the week let every one of you lay by him in store, as God hath prospered him. [Hence the custom of offerings for the poor, and contributions for benevolent objects, on Sundays, as a part of public worship.]

Rev. 1, 10. I was in the Spirit on the Lord's day.

These passages prove the *apostolic practice*, which is further confirmed by the universal custom of the Christian Church from the second century down to the present. This practice rests upon the divine *fact* of the *resurrection* of Christ, which took place on the first day of the week (Matt. 28, 1), as also on the fact that Christ *appeared* to the assembled disciples on the same and the following Sunday, to bless them, and on the fact of the *outpouring of the Holy Ghost* and the *founding of the Christian Church* on the fiftieth day, or seventh Sunday, after the resurrection.

7. *What is the design and use of the Lord's Day?*

To maintain public worship, to give rest to body and soul, and to prepare us for the eternal sabbath in heaven.

Heb. 4, 9. There remaineth therefore a rest [Greek, *sabbatismos, i.e.* keeping of a sabbath, or an eternal rest with God] to the people of God.

NOTES AND HINTS.

NAMES of the holy day of the week: (1.) *Sabbath, i.e.* day of rest,—not a rest of idleness, but a rest of benediction and perfection on the part of God (Gen. 2, 3; John 5, 17), and a rest *in* God on the part of the creature, which is made for God, and "remains without rest, until it rests in God." We should cease on the Lord's Day from our own work, that God may do his work in us. The name *sabbath* is used in the Bible of the *Jewish* sabbath, or *seventh* day of the week, but may with full propriety be retained for the Christian sabbath, or Sunday, as is the custom especially among Christians of the English tongue.

(2.) *The Lord's day*, i. e. the day exclusively devoted to the memory and service of our Lord and Saviour, who rose on that day, Rev. 1, 10. This term was first used by John, the favorite disciple, the apostle, evangelist, and seer of the New Testament. It occurs only of the *Christian* sabbath, or the *first* day of the week, and is the best and most significant name for the Christian Sabbath.

(3.) *Sunday*, i. e. day of the sun (dedicated to the god of the sun among the heathen), is, like the names of the week-days, of heathen origin, but we now give it a reference to Christ as the true Sun of righteousness and the Light of the world.

ORIGIN.—The sabbath is older than Moses and the Jewish religion, and, like the institution of marriage and the family, goes back even beyond the fall, to the primitive state of innocence in paradise, Gen. 2, 2. 3. Hence the word "*remember* the sabbath day," which presupposes its previous existence and observance, however much for a long time it may have been neglected. Hence also the traces of the hebdomadal division with a weekly holy day, which are found among ancient nations, especially of the Semitic race, and which are as many reminiscences of the original institution. Being grounded in the original constitution of man, the sabbath must have universal and permanent significance. It was, therefore, as little abolished by Christ as any other part of the decalogue, but only fulfilled and perfected, like the rest, acccording to the general principle laid down in Matt. 5, 17. 18. Had the sabbath been intended merely for the Jews, like the ceremonial laws, it would never have found a place in the decalogue. We might as well say that Christ abolished the law against swearing, against murder, against adultery, against theft, as to say that he abolished the fourth commandment. They all hang together as an inseparable unit and complete whole.

AUTHORITY and permanent OBLIGATION.—This must not be based exclusively on the law (the legalistic or sabbatarian theory); nor exclusively on the resurrection of Christ (the merely evangelical or dominical theory); nor on the authority of the Christian Church (the ecclesiastical or traditional theory); but on the *combined authority of the Old and New Testament*, the *law* and the *gospel*, to which the *Church* is bound. In other words, the sabbath rests (1) on the primitive creation and the universal want of man for periodical rest of body and soul (Gen. 2, 3. 4; Ex. 20, 11; Mark 2, 27); (2) on the Old Testament legislation, or the fourth commandment of the decalogue, which, in all its parts, is still binding upon all Christians (Matt. 5, 17–20); (3) on the fact of Christ's resurrection and the practice of the Apostolic Church (Acts 20, 7; 1 Cor. 16, 2; Rev. 1, 10). The first and second grounds secure the universal and perpetual obligation of the sabbath; the last ground justifies the change of day, and points to the proper spirit in the mode of its observance.

OBJECT.—The sabbath was made for the benefit of man (Mark 2, 27), and is necessary for his physical, moral, and spiritual well-being. The law clearly points out this benevolent design, and extends it to the servant, and the poor stranger or heathen sojourning among the Jews, yea, even to irrational cattle.—Comp. Ex. 23, 12 (that thine ox and thine ass may rest, and the son of thy handmaid, and the stranger, may be refreshed).

Q. 3. As love is the fulfilment of the whole law, works of love to

God (acts of worship), and works of charity to our fellow-men, are the best observance of the law on the sabbath.

Q. 4. The passages quoted mostly refer to the observance of the *Jewish* sabbath, or the *seventh* day, and are, therefore, only *indirect* proofs. But the Christian's obligation properly to observe the Lord's day exceeds that of the Jew in proportion to the blessings he receives and commemorates.

Q. 6. The *change of the day* does not affect the essence and permanent obligation of the law on the sabbath, but is a mere matter of form. We must distinguish in the fourth commandment the moral from the ceremonial part. The abiding moral substance is that at least *one day out of seven days* be kept holy and devoted exclusively to the service of God, while six days may and ought to be employed in useful work; the temporary ceremonial form is that the *seventh* day of the week be set apart for this sacred purpose. The *seventh* day, or the *Jewish* sabbath, was commemorative of the *natural* creation, and at the same time of the *typical* redemption from the bondage of Egypt (which is expressly connected with the sabbath law in Deut. 5, 15); the *first* day of the week, or the *Christian* sabbath, reminds us of the *spiritual* creation, and *complete* redemption from the bondage of sin and death by the resurrection of the Saviour. The Jewish sabbath was buried with Christ as to its national and typical form, and rose with him under a higher spiritual form as the Lord's Day, or "the day of the Lord," divested of the bondage of legalism, a free evangelical feast of the spirit in grateful joy in the accomplished redemption and its unspeakable blessings. The Lord's Day connects the commemoration of creation and redemption, the paradise lost and the paradise regained, and is a pledge and foretaste of the saint's everlasting rest in heaven (Heb. 4, 9–11).

Q. 7. Rest in God is the *end of all creation*: comp. Heb. 3, 11; 4, 1–11. This is the rest, not of inaction, but of perfection, which includes the highest spiritual activity and enjoyment in unbbroken peace and harmony. So God rested on the seventh day by completing and blessing the creation. The beginning of history foreshadows its end. Every sabbath on earth is a preparation for, and foretaste of, the eternal sabbath in heaven, or heaven itself let down from week to week, that we may breathe its air, behold its light, hear its music, join in its worship, and enjoy its peace. The sabbath has, therefore, been called "the pearl of days," and "the light of the week:" without it life is a journey through a dreary wilderness, with no prospect of a land of promise.

XLVI. The Fifth Commandment.

1. *What is the fifth commandment?*

Honor thy father and thy mother: that thy days may be long upon the land which the Lord thy God giveth thee.

Ex. 20, 12.—Deut. 5, 16. Comp. Eph. 6, 2.

2. What does God enjoin in this commandment?

That we cheerfully render to our parents, teachers, and other superiors, all due honor, love, and obedience in the Lord.

(1.) Duties of *children* to parents and their representatives (guardians): * Prov. 1, 8. 9. My son, hear the instruction of thy father, and forsake not the law of thy mother; for they shall be an ornament of grace unto thy head, and chains about thy neck.—Comp. 4, 1; 6, 20-23; 23, 22. 25. * Eph. 6, 1-3. Children, obey your parents in the Lord: for this is right. Honor thy father and thy mother; which is the first commandment with promise; that it may be well with thee, and thou mayest live long on the earth.—Col. 3, 20. Children, obey your parents in all things: for this is well pleasing unto the Lord.—Comp. the *example* of Christ: Luke 2, 51.

(2.) Duties of *servants* to masters: Col. 3, 22. 23. Servants, obey in all things your masters according to the flesh; not with eye-service, as men-pleasers; but in singleness of heart, fearing God. And whatsoever ye do, do it heartily, as to the Lord, and not unto men.—Comp. Eph. 6, 5-8; 1 Tim. 6, 1. 2; Tit. 2, 9. 10; 1 Pet. 2, 18.

(3.) Duties of *pupils* to teachers, and of *church-members* to their pastors: Heb. 13, 17. Obey them that have the rule over you, and submit yourselves: for they watch for your souls, as they that must give account, that they may do it with joy, and not with grief.—Comp. 1 Thess. 5, 12. 13; 1 Tim. 5, 17; Phil. 2, 29; Matt. 23, 3.

(4.) Duties of *subjects* to magistrates: Matt. 22, 21. Render unto Cæsar the things that are Cæsar's.—Rom. 13, 1. Let every soul be subject unto the higher powers. For there is no power but of God: the powers that be are ordained of God.—Comp. Tit. 3, 1; 1 Pet. 2, 13. 14. 17.

(5.) Duties of the *young* to the aged: Lev. 19, 32. Thou shalt rise up before the hoary head, and honor the face of the old man, and fear thy God.—1 Pet. 5, 5. Ye younger, submit yourselves unto the elder.—Comp. 1 Tim. 5, 1-3

3. What is forbidden in this commandment?

All disrespect, disobedience, or neglect of our parents, teachers, or any other superiors.

Lev. 20, 9. Every one that curseth his father or his mother shall be surely put to death.

Deut. 27, 16. Cursed be he that setteth light by his father or his mother. And all the people shall say, Amen.
Ex. 22, 28. Thou shalt not revile the judges, nor curse the ruler of thy people.—Comp. Prov. 20, 20; 30, 17; Matt. 15, 4.

4. What are the duties of parents?

To bring up their children in the nurture and admonition of the Lord, for usefulness in this world, and for eternal happiness in the world to come.

* **Prov. 22, 6.** Train up a child in the way he should go: and when he is old, he will not depart from it.
Eph. 6, 4. Ye fathers, provoke not your children to wrath, but bring them up in the nurture and admonition of the Lord.
Comp. Col. 3, 21; Deut. 6, 6–9; Prov. 23, 13. 14; 29, 17.

5. What are the duties of superiors in general?

To promote, both by precept and example, the temporal and spiritual welfare of those intrusted to their care.

(1.) Duties of *masters* to servants: Col. 4, 1. Masters, give unto your servants that which is just and equal; knowing that ye also have a Master in heaven.—Comp. Eph. 6, 9; Lev. 25, 43.

(2.) Duties of *pastors* to their flock: John 21, 15–17. Feed my lambs. ... Feed my sheep.—Comp. Acts 20, 28; 1 Cor. 9, 27; 1 Pet. 5, 1–3.

(3.) Duties of *magistrates* to subjects: Rom. 13, 3. 4. Rulers are not a terror to good works, but to the evil. ... He is the minister of God to thee for good.—Comp. 1. Pet. 2, 14; Deut. 5, 19. 20; Ps. 2, 10. 11; Ex. 18, 21. 22; 2 Chr. 19, 6. 7.

EXAMPLES of pious rulers and kings: Moses, Joshua, Samuel, David, Solomon (in his first period), Hezekiah, Josiah. Bad kings: Rehoboam, Ahab, Manasseh, Herod, etc.

6. Why does God add a special promise to this commandment?

Because the family is the foundation of society, and obedience to parents is the condition of all true happiness and prosperity.

NOTES AND HINTS.

Q. 1. The fifth commandment is usually placed in the *second* table, among the duties to our neighbor. But the Jews and the Christian

Fathers equally divided the two tables. Josephus says (Antiq. Book III. ch. 6, § 5): "In this ark [of the covenant] he [Moses] put the two tables whereon the ten commandments were written, five upon each table, and two and a half upon each side of them; and this ark he placed in the holy of holies." St. Paul, in enumerating the commandments of the second table, or of love to our neighbor, omits the fifth, Rom. 13, 9, which indicates that he placed it likewise in the first table. This division accords best with the law of symmetry, and the significance of the number ten,—the union of two equal halves. Parents, moreover, are not so much our neighbors as our superiors, and visible representatives of divine authority on earth. Hence they are not simply to be loved, like our neighbor, but also to be *honored* and *obeyed*. In honoring them we honor God to whom properly all honor is due (comp. the first and second commandments and Ps. 115, 1; Is. 42, 8); while men can only claim honor and obedience as representing his authority. It should be noticed also that the words: *the Lord thy God*, are repeated here as in all the commandments of the first table, while they are omitted in those of the second which relate to our neighbor. For these reasons, the fifth commandment belongs rather to the first table, and forms the transition from our duties to God to our duties to man. It embraces, however, according to the wide latitude of the names of father and mother in the Scriptures (comp. Gen. 45, 8; Judg. 5, 7), the duties to all our superiors, or those who have authority over us, whether spiritual or temporal (comp. Ex. 22, 28). For all authority is ordained by God and an emanation of his absolute sovereignty (Rom. 13, 1). The relation between parents and children underlies all divinely constituted relations of superiority and inferiority. The family is the primitive order of society and the nursery of church and state. From the family to the school; from the school to the church; and from the church to heaven.

According to this division (which is adopted also by several distinguished modern commentators of the Old Testament, as Hengstenberg, of Germany, and Fairbairn, of Scotland), the order and gradation of the successive commands of the first table is this: Love God above all things, and give him the honor and glory due to him, (1) in regard to his *being*, as the only true and living God; (2) in regard to his *worship*; (3) in regard to his *name*, or the outward manifestation of his being; (4) in regard to his *day* of holy rest; (5) in regard to his *representatives* on earth who are clothed with his authority.

Q. 2. The boundary of all obedience to *human* authority is obedience to *divine* authority. For we must obey God rather than men, Acts 5, 29; Matt. 10, 37. Hence obedience to parents, rulers, etc. is qualified by the phrase: *in the Lord*.

Q. 6. Obedience to rightful authority is the mother of virtue and of true freedom; disobedience (the sin of Adam and Eve) is the mother of sin and of slavery. The promise of the fifth commandment has special reference to the possession of the promised land. But this was a type of the heavenly Canaan to which Christians look forward as their final and true home. Long life in this world is, therefore, not the *only* reward of obedience. God may at times better promote the eternal happiness of a child by transplanting him, in early youth, from this world of temptation and trial to the better world of holiness and peace. In Deut. 5, 16 and Eph. 6, 3 the promise of long life is qualified by the additional words: "*that it may go well with thee*." Welfare or true well being is the chief reward, without which a long life on earth would only be a long evil.

XLVII. The Sixth Commandment.

1. *Of what do the last five commandments treat?*

Of love to our neighbor.

Rom. 13, 9. For this, Thou shalt not commit adultery, Thou shalt not kill, Thou shalt not steal, Thou shalt not bear false witness, Thou shalt not covet, . . . is briefly comprehended in this saying, namely, Thou shalt love thy neighbor as thyself.

1 John 4, 20. If a man say, I love God, and hateth his brother, he is a liar: for he that loveth not his brother whom he hath seen, how can he love God whom he hath not seen?

2. *Who is your neighbor?*

Every man with whom we come in contact, and to whom we can do good, without distinction of race, character, or condition.

Gen. 1, 27; Acts 17, 26.—Eph. 4, 4–6.
Comp. the parable of the good Samaritan, Luke 10, 29–37.

3. *What is the sum of your duties to your neighbor?*

To love him as myself, and to do unto him as I wish him to do unto me.

* Matt. 22, 39. Thou shalt love thy neighbor as thyself.—Comp. Lev. 19, 18.

* Matt. 7, 12. Whatsoever ye would that men should do to you, do ye even so to them: for this is the law and the prophets.—Comp. Luke 6, 31.

4. *What is the sixth commandment?*

Thou shalt not kill.

Ex. 20, 13.—Deut. 5, 17; Matt. 5, 21.

5. *What is forbidden in this commandment?*

Murder and suicide, or the wilful destruction of human life, whether it be done by our own hands, or by the agency of another.

Examples of *murderers:* Cain, Gen. 4, 8; comp. 1 John 3, 12; Joab, 2 Sam. 3, 27; 20, 10; Zimri, 1 Kings 16, 10; Ahab, 1 Kings 21, 18. 19; Herodias, Mark 6, 19-28.

Examples of *suicide:* Abimelech, Judg. 9, 54: Saul, 1 Sam. 31, 4; Ahithophel, 2 Sam. 17, 23; Zimri, 1 Kings 16, 18; Judas Iscariot, Matt. 27, 5.—Suicide condemned, Acts 16, 28.

6. *Who alone has a right to take human life?*

The magistrate, who, as the minister of God, bears the sword for the punishment of evil-doers.

Gen. 9, 6. Whoso sheddeth man's blood, by man shall his blood be shed: for in the image of God made he man.
Lev. 24, 17; Deut. 19, 11-13; Rom. 13, 4.

7. *Why are we forbidden to destroy human life?*

Because God alone is lord over life and death, and because man is made in the image of God, and is our brother.

Gen. 9, 5. 6; James 3, 9.—1 Cor. 3, 16. 17; 6, 20.

8. *What else is forbidden in this commandment?*

All provoking words, and feelings of envy, hatred, wrath, and revenge towards our neighbor.

Lev. 19, 17. Thou shalt not hate thy brother in thine heart.

Matt. 5, 22. Whosoever is angry with his brother without a cause, shall be in danger of the judgment [*i.e.* the local magistrate of the seven, established in every town, Deut. 16, 18]: and whosoever shall say to his brother, Raca [vain fellow], shall be in danger of the council [*i.e.* the Sanhedrim, or higher tribunal of the seventy in Jerusalem, Luke 22, 66; Acts 5, 21]: but whosoever shall say, Thou fool [wicked fellow, comp. Ps. 14, 1], shall be in danger of hell-fire [gehenna, place of condemnation].

* 1 John 3, 15. Whosoever hateth his brother is a murderer.

* Eph. 4, 31. Let all bitterness, and wrath, and anger, and clamor, and evil speaking, be put away from you, with all malice.

Rom. 12, 19. Avenge not yourselves, but rather give place unto wrath [to the wrath of God]: for it is written, Vengeance is mine; I will repay, saith the Lord (Deut. 32, 35).

THE SIXTH COMMANDMENT.

Prov. 16, 32. He that is slow to anger is better than the mighty; and he that ruleth his spirit, than he that taketh a city.

James 1, 19; 1 Pet. 2, 1; Rom. 1, 29; Col. 3, 8; Gal. 5, 19-21; 1 Cor. 3, 3; Prov. 15, 1; 16, 32.

9. *What duties are required in the sixth commandment?*

That we have a sacred regard for the life of our neighbor and for our own, cheerfully assist him in all distress, and return good for evil even to our enemies.

* 1 Cor. 3, 16. Know ye not that ye are the temple of God, and that the Spirit of God dwelleth in you?

1 Cor. 6, 20. Glorify God in your body, and in your spirit, which are God's.

Rom. 12, 10. Be kindly affectioned one to another with brotherly love, in honor preferring one another.

* Rom. 12, 20. 21. If thine enemy hunger, feed him; if he thirst, give him drink: for in so doing thou shalt heap coals of fire on his head. Be not overcome of evil, but overcome evil with good.

Col. 3, 12. 13. Put on ... bowels of mercies, kindness, humbleness of mind, meekness, long-suffering; forbearing one another, and forgiving one another, if any man have a quarrel against any: even as Christ forgave you, so also do ye.

Ps. 133, 1. Behold, how good and how pleasant it is for brethren to dwell together in unity.

1 John 3, 17. 18; James 2, 15. 16; Heb. 13, 1-3; Acts 20, 35; Matt. 5, 44.

NOTES AND HINTS.

Q. 1. Love to God and love to man are as inseparable as cause and effect: hence the Lord joins them together, Matt. 22, 39. The first table contains our religious duties, the second our moral duties. Religion is the source of morality. We must first stand in right relation to God, before we can properly act our part to our fellow-creatures. Love and obedience to God is the parent and guardian of all social and private virtues.

The second table teaches also the duties *to ourselves.* For if we are required to love our neighbor *as ourselves,* it is implied that we should love ourselves. Both in us and in our neighbor we are not to love sin or weakness, but the *image of God,* in which man is made. Hence true love to ourselves and to our fellow men can in no wise conflict with our love to God, but is, in its essence, one and the same.

THE SIXTH COMMANDMENT.

The first table proceeds from the *heart* (first and second commandments), to *words* (third), and *deeds* (fourth and fifth commandments); the second table follows the reverse order, from *deeds* (sixth, seventh, and eighth), and *words* (ninth), to the *heart* (tenth). The tenth and the first commandments meet in the *heart*, the secret source of all disobedience or obedience to the will of God, as it is filled either with selfishness, in its corrupt natural state, or with love to God and man, in its regenerate state.

Q. 2. *Neighbor* (from nigh, near), in the strict sense, means one who is united to us by the ties of kindred (Lev. 25, 25), or friendship (Job 19, 14; Ps. 38, 12), or nation and country. But even in the Old Testament the Egyptian is called the neighbor of the Hebrew (Ex. 11, 2), and in the New Testament the term is extended to every fellow-man who needs our help, or to whom we have an opportunity of doing good, though he be of a different race and a different religion. See the parable of the good Samaritan, Luke 10, 29–37. There is, however, a difference between love to man in general, including even an enemy (Matt. 5, 44; Rom. 12, 20. 21), and love to the brethren of the same faith, Gal. 6, 10; 2 Pet. 1, 7. While we should do good to all men, whenever God gives us an opportunity, we should nevertheless avoid intercourse and familiarity with the enemies of religion and good morals, 2 Cor. 6, 14–17; 2 John 10.

Q. 3. The propriety and beauty of our Saviours' rule that we should do unto others as we would have them do unto us, is so evident to reason and sound sense, that even unbelievers must approve and admire it. The heathen emperor Alexander Severus (a. 222–235), whose mother, Julia Mammæa, was favorably inclined to Christianity, caused this rule, Luke 7, 31, to be inscribed on the walls of his palace and on public monuments. But the natural man can at best only live up to the *negative* part of this rule, by abstaining from injuring his neighbor. Our Saviour requires that we should do positive good to our neighbor, and this can be done only by a heart filled with the love of God and of Christ.

Q. 4. The sixth commandment treats of our duties to the *life* of our neighbor which includes his soul and body. Hence it condemns also all injury to the soul of man by poisoning his mind with false and pernicious teaching.

Q. 5. Wanton exposure to danger is a sin, Matt. 4, 6. 7; Deut. 6, 6 (Ye shall not tempt the Lord your God); but cheerful readiness to die for Christ and for truth, is a duty and virtue, and martyrdom, the greatest honor, John 15, 12. 13; 1 John 3, 16 (We ought to lay down our lives for the brethren).

There is also a *gradual* suicide, by intemperance in meat and drink and other vices which undermine health. Against the vice of *intemperance*, see Luke 21, 34. Take heed to yourselves, lest at any time your hearts be overcharged with surfeiting, and drunkenness, and cares of this life. Rom. 13, 13. Let us walk honestly, as in the day; not in rioting and drunkenness. Eph. 5, 18. Be not drunk with wine, wherein is excess; but be filled with the Spirit. 1 Pet. 4, 3; Prov. 23, 31–33.

Q. 6. The responsibility of killing enemies in legitimate war rests likewise with the magistrate or government which carries on the war. Killing a man in necessary self-defence, or preventing the murder of the innocent by killing the guilty, is justifiable by the law of nature and of nations (comp. also Ex. 22, 2. 3; Numb. 35, 27); yet the Christian, before resorting to such extreme remedy, should carefully weigh the words of Christ, Matt. 5, 38–45, and the example of his innocent suffering. Wars in national *self-defense* against foreign invasion or domestic rebellion are unavoidable in the present corrupt state of society; but wars of *conquest* are always wrong, and sooner or later visited with divine punishment.

Q. 8. Hatred is secret murder of the heart, and the mother of the deed, 1 John 3, 15. So there is also an adultery of the heart, which is already a sin before God, Matt. 5, 28.

XLVIII. The Seventh Commandment.

1. *What is the seventh commandment?*

Thou shalt not commit adultery.

Exod. 20, 14.—Deut. 5, 18; Matt. 5, 27.

2. *What does God forbid in this commandment?*

All unchastity in thought, gesture, word, or deed, whether in or out of married life.

(1.) Unclean *desires* and *looks* (secret adultery of the *heart*): Matt. 5, 28. Whosoever looketh on a woman to lust after her, hath committed adultery with her already in his heart.— Comp. Matt. 15, 19 (out of the heart proceed . . . adulteries, fornications).

(2.) Unclean *words* and *gestures:* Eph. 4, 29. Let no corrupt communication proceed out of your mouth.—Comp. 5, 3. 4; Col. 3, 8 (filthy communication out of your mouth).

(3.) Unclean *actions:* 1 Cor. 6, 18. Flee fornication. Every sin that a man doeth is without the body; but he that committeth fornication sinneth against his own body. Gal. 5, 19. The works of the flesh are manifest, which are these: Adultery, fornication, uncleanness, lasciviousness, etc.—Col. 3, 5; Eph. 5, 5 (no whoremonger, nor unclean person, . . . hath any inheritance in the kingdom of Christ); 1 Thess. 4, 3. 4; Heb. 13, 4; Rev. 21, 8.

3. *What else is here forbidden?*

Bad company, intemperance in meat and drink, luxury and idleness, filthy conversation, obscene books, songs, and pictures, and whatsoever excites unchaste desires.

* 1 Cor. 15, 33. Evil communications corrupt good manners.
* 2 Tim. 2, 22. Flee youthful lusts.

Rom. 13, 12-14. Let us cast off the works of darkness, and let us put on the armor of light. Let us walk honestly, as in the day; not in rioting and drunkenness, not in chamber-

THE SEVENTH COMMANDMENT. 155

ing and wantonness, not in strife and envying. But put ye on the Lord Jesus Christ, and make not provision for the flesh, to fulfil the lusts thereof.

Eph. 5, 3. 4. But fornication, and all uncleanness, or covetousness, let it not be once named among you, as becometh saints; neither filthiness, nor foolish talking, nor jesting, which are not convenient [becoming].

4. *Why is unchastity such a heinous sin?*

Because by unchastity we dishonor and corrupt our body and soul, which are the temple of the Holy Ghost.

* 1 Cor. 3, 16. 17. Know ye not that ye are the temple of God, and that the Spirit of God dwelleth in you? If any man defile the temple of God, him shall God destroy; for the temple of God is holy, which temple ye are.

1 Cor. 6, 18–20; Eph. 5, 5; Rev. 22, 15; Lev. 20, 10.

5. *What does God require in this commandment?*

To be chaste and temperate, whether in the married or single state, and to keep our body pure, as a temple of the Holy Ghost.

1 Cor. 3, 16. 17; 6, 18–20; Matt. 5, 8; Heb. 13, 4.

EXAMPLE of chastity under great temptation: Joseph in the house of Potiphar, Gen. 39, 9: "How can I do this great wickedness, and sin against God?"

6. *What does God especially enjoin upon married persons?*

Mutual esteem, love, and fidelity unto death.

Eph. 5, 22–31; Col. 3, 18. 19; 1 Pet. 3, 1–6.

7. *What is marriage?*

An inseparable union of life in love between one man and one woman, instituted by God in paradise, and reflecting the mystical union between Christ and his Church.

Gen. 1, 27; 2, 18; Matt. 19, 5. 6; Eph. 5, 31. 32.

Duties of husbands and wives to each other: Eph. 5, 22–29; Col. 3, 18. 19; 1 Pet. 3, 1–7.

8. For what purpose has God instituted marriage?

For the mutual aid and happiness of married persons, for the propagation of the race, and for the building up of the kingdom of God through Christian nurture.

Gen. 1, 28; 2, 18; Eph. 6, 4; Heb. 13, 4; 1 Tim. 4, 1–3.

NOTES AND HINTS.

Q. 7. Polygamy, which is allowed among heathens, Mohammedans, and Mormons, was never sanctioned in the Old Testament, but simply tolerated on account of hardness of heart, until the advent of Christ. It is in direct contradiction to the institution of marriage as recorded in Genesis, and destroys the dignity of woman by degrading her to a mere slave. God gave to Adam only one wife and took her from his rib, "not out of his head, to top him—not out of his feet, to be trampled upon by him—but out of his side, to be equal with him—from under his arm, to be protected—and from near his heart, to be beloved." Lamech, of the race of Cain, gave the first example of polygamy, Gen. 4, 19. Christianity restored monogamy as the only normal form of marriage, elevated woman to her present noble position in society, and has laid her under especial obligations of gratitude. This elevation of woman to moral and religious equality with man, and to joint-heirship of heaven, lies at the foundation of true family happiness, and the Christian training of children. Woman owes everything to Christianity, and cannot be sufficiently thankful for the blessings and privileges she enjoys in Christian lands, as compared with her wretched and helpless condition among ancient and modern heathens (even the Chinese, Japanese, and Hindoos), and Mohammedans.

Q. 7 and 8 may be omitted by the teacher. The whole subject of the seventh commandment should be handled with wise caution, yet with great earnestness.

XLIX. The Eighth Commandment.

1. What is the eighth commandment?

Thou shalt not steal.

Exod. 20, 15.—Deut. 5, 19; Matt. 19, 18.

2. What does God forbid in this commandment?

Robbery, theft, fraud, and all injury to the property of our neighbor.

Lev. 19, 11. Ye shall not steal, neither deal falsely.
Eph. 4, 28. Let him that stole, steal no more.
1 Thess. 4, 6. That no man go beyond and defraud his

brother in any matter; because that the Lord is the avenger of all such.
1 Pet. 4, 15. Let none of you suffer as a murderer, or as a thief, or as an evildoer, or as a busybody in other men's matters.
Ps. 37, 21. The wicked borroweth, and payeth not again: but the righteous showeth mercy and giveth.
Lev. 19, 13. 35. 36; Jer. 22, 13; Hab. 2, 6. 9; James 5, 4; 1 Pet. 4, 15; 1 Cor. 6, 10.

3. *What other sins are here prohibited?*

Idleness, covetousness, wastefulness, and whatever may lead to theft and fraud.

(1.) Against *idleness* ("the devil's workshop"): * 2 Thess. 3, 10. If any would not work, neither should he eat.—1 Thess. 4, 11; Eph. 4, 28; Gen. 3, 19.

(2.) Against *covetousness* and *avarice*, or undue love of money: * Matt. 6, 24. Ye cannot serve God and mammon. *1 Tim. 6, 10. The love of money is the root [literally, *a* root] of all evil.—Comp. Matt. 6, 31. 32; Luke 12, 15; Eph. 5, 5; Col. 3, 5; Heb. 13, 5; 1 Tim. 6, 7-10; 1 John 2, 15. 16; Ps. 62, 10 (If riches increase, set not your heart upon them).—EXAMPLE: Judas, who from covetousness became a thief and a traitor.

Riches in themselves are a gift of God, and to possess them is no more sin than to possess beauty, or strength, or genius. But we should never set our heart upon riches (Ps. 62, 10) nor serve them (Matt. 6, 24), but rather make them serve us for good purposes, as those who have to render an account.—EXAMPLES of rich servants of God: Abraham, Job, David, and other pious kings of Israel.

(3.) Against *wastefulness* and *extravagance*, or wanton disregard of earthly goods: Prov. 21, 17. He that loveth pleasure shall be a poor man; he that loveth wine and oil shall not be rich. Prov. 12, 27; 23, 20. 21; 28, 19.—EXAMPLE: The prodigal son in the parable, who wasted his substance with riotous living, Luke 15, 13. 14.

The proper *medium* between the two opposite vices of covetousness and prodigality is the virtue of *economy* which looks to our own support and the benefit of our neighbor. Prov. 13, 22. A good man leaveth an inheritance to his children's children. 1 Tim. 5, 8. If any provide not for his own, and specially for those of his own house, he hath denied the faith, and is worse than an infidel. John 6, 12. Gather up the fragments that remain, that nothing be lost.—(John Wesley's maxim: "Make all you can, save all you can, give all you can.")

THE EIGHTH COMMANDMENT.

4. What are the duties enjoined in the eighth commandment?

Labor and industry, honesty and fidelity in our dealings, contentment with our lot, kindness and liberality to our neighbor.

(1.) *Labor* and *industry:* * Eph. 4, 28. Let him labor, working with his hand the thing which is good, that he may have to give to him that needeth. Prov. 13, 11. Wealth gotten by vanity shall be diminished: but he that gathered by labor shall increase.—Gen. 3, 19; 1 Thess. 4, 11; 2 Thess. 3, 10–12; Acts 20, 34.

(2.) *Honesty* and *faithfulness:* Luke 16, 10. He that is faithful in that which is least is faithful also in much: and he that is unjust in the least is unjust also in much. * Matt. 25, 21. Well done, thou good and faithful servant: thou hast been faithful over a few things, I will make thee ruler over many things: enter thou into the joy of thy lord. 1 Cor. 10, 24. Let no man seek his own, but every man another's wealth. Phil. 2, 4. Look not every man on his own things, but every man also on the things of others.—Deut. 22, 1–3.— EXAMPLE: Zaccheus, who gave the half of his goods to the poor, and restored unjust gains fourfold, Luke 19, 8.

(3.) *Contentment:* * 1 Tim. 6, 6. 8. Godliness with contentment is great gain. . . . Having food and raiment, let us be therewith content. Heb. 13, 5. Be content with such things as ye have: for he hath said, I will never leave thee nor forsake thee.—Gen. 28, 15; Deut. 31, 6; Ps. 37, 25; Phil. 4, 11–13.

(4.) *Benevolence* and *liberality:* Matt. 5, 42. Give to him that asketh thee, and from him that would borrow of thee turn not thou away. * Acts 20, 35. It is more blessed to give than to receive. Gal. 5, 13. By love serve one another. * Heb. 13, 16. To do good and to communicate forget not; for with such sacrifices God is well pleased.—Comp. Matt. 25, 35, 36; Rom. 12, 13. 20; 2 Cor. 9, 7; Heb. 13, 1–3.—EXAMPLES: Zaccheus, Luke 19, 8; the poor widow in the temple, Mark 12, 41–44; the first Christians at Jerusalem, Acts 4, 34–37.

NOTE.

Q. 2. The eighth commandment forbids all sins against the *property* of our neighbor, not only by violent robbery or secret theft, but also by any kind of direct or indirect fraud, such as false coins, weights, and measures (Lev. 19, 35. 36; Deut. 15, 13; Prov. 11, 1; 22, 10); usury, or unlawful interest (Exod. 22, 25; Ps. 15, 5); extortion (Ezek. 22, 12; Matt. 23, 25; 1 Cor. 6, 10); oppression (Lev. 25, 17; Luke 3, 14); removing landmarks (Deut. 19, 14); concealment of stolen goods, or connivance at theft (Prov. 29, 24); unfaithfulness in contracts, or in matters of trust (Amos 8, 5: Luke 16, 11); bribery (Job 15, 34; Isa. 33. 15); withholding or curtailing of wages (Lev. 19, 13; Deut. 24, 14. 15; James

5, 4); fondness for litigation (Prov. 3, 30; 1 Cor. 6, 7); wanton borrowing (Ps. 37, 21); withholding tribute from government (Matt. 22, 21; Rom. 13, 7); unnecessary delay in paying just debts (as the minister's salary); smuggling, lazy begging, prodigality, gambling, jugglery, and all kinds of dishonest or doubtful dealings, wicked tricks and devices, whereby we design to enrich ourselves at the expense and to the injury of our neighbor.

L. The Ninth Commandment.

1. *What is the ninth commandment?*

Thou shalt not bear false witness against thy neighbor.

Exod. 20, 16.—Deut. 5, 20.

2. *What does God forbid in this commandment?*

Not only false testimony before a court of justice, but also lying, slander, uncharitable judgment, and whatever tends to injure the good name of our neighbor.

(1.) Against *false testimony* before the magistrate: Prov. 21, 28. A false witness shall perish. Exod. 23, 1; Deut. 19, 16–19; Prov. 19, 5. 9. 28.

(2.) Against *falsehood* and *slander* generally: Lev. 19, 11. Ye shall not... lie one to another. * Eph. 4, 25. Putting away lying, speak every man truth with his neighbor. 1 Pet. 3, 10. He that will love life, and see good days, let him refrain his tongue from evil, and his lips that they speak no guile.—Ps. 5, 6; Matt. 15, 19; Col. 3, 9; 1 Pet. 2, 1; 1 Cor. 6, 10; Rev. 21, 8; 22, 15.

(3.) Against *rash* and *uncharitable judgment:* Matt. 7, 1, 2. Judge not, that ye be not judged. For with what judgment ye judge, ye shall be judged: and with what measure ye mete, it shall be measured to you again. Luke 6, 37. Judge not, and ye shall not be judged: condemn not, and ye shall not be condemned: forgive, and ye shall be forgiven.—Rom. 2, 1; 14, 3. 4. 10. 13; 1 Cor. 4, 5; James 4, 11. 12.

3. *Why is lying such a great sin?*

Because God is a God of truth, and lies come from the devil, the father of lies.

John 8, 44. When he [the devil] speaketh a lie, he speaketh of his own: for he is a liar, and the father of it.
Ps. 31, 5. (Lord God of truth); Deut. 32, 4 (A God of truth and without iniquity, just and right is he); Jer. 10, 10 (Heb.: God is truth); John 14, 6 (I am the truth).

4. *What are the duties required in this commandment?*

Truthfulness, honesty, good faith to our neighbor, and a sacred regard for his character and good name.

* Zech. 8, 16. 17. Speak ye every man the truth to his neighbor, . . . and let none of you imagine evil in your hearts against his neighbor.
1 Pet. 4, 8. Above all things, have fervent charity among yourselves: for charity shall cover the [lit., a] multitude of sins.
Eph. 4, 15. Speaking the truth in love.
Ps. 15, 1–3; Prov. 12, 19; Eph. 4, 25; 1 Cor. 13, 6; 1 Pet. 4, 8.

5. *Is it ever lawful to speak an untruth?*

No: all that we say must be true; but we may sometimes withhold the truth for the good of our neighbor.

John 16, 12. I have yet many things to say unto you, but ye cannot bear them now.
* Prov. 29, 11. A fool uttereth all his mind: but a wise man keepeth it in till afterwards.

6. *What is your duty concerning your own name?*

I should keep my name pure and blameless, and avoid even the appearance of evil.

* Prov. 22, 1. A good name is rather to be chosen than great riches, and loving favor rather than silver and gold.
Eccles. 7, 1. A good name is better than precious ointment.
1 Cor. 9, 15. It were better for me to die, than that any man should make my glorying void. [Comp. however, 1 Cor. 15, 9. 10. By the grace of God I am what I am; and Gal. 6, 14. God forbid that I should glory, save in the cross of our Lord Jesus Christ.]
* 1 Thess. 5, 22. Abstain from all appearance of evil.
Phil. 4, 8. Whatsoever things are true, whatsoever things

are honest [literally, venerable, honorable], whatsoever things are just, whatsoever things are pure, whatsoever things are lovely, whatsoever things are of good report; if there be any virtue, and if there be any praise, think on these things.

7. *Is it lawful to indulge in pride and vanity?*

No: pride is sin, vanity a weakness, and self-praise folly; but humility which gives all glory to God, is the chief grace and ornament of a Christian.

* Rom. 12, 16. Be not wise in your own conceits.

Phil. 2, 3. In lowliness of mind let each esteem other better than themselves.

Prov. 27, 2. Let another man praise thee, and not thine own mouth; a stranger, and not thine own lips.

* 1 Pet. 5, 5. Be clothed with humility: for God resisteth the proud, and giveth grace to the humble.

1 Cor. 15, 9. 10. I am the least of the apostles, that am not meet to be called an apostle, because I persecuted the church of God. But by the grace of God I am what I am: and his grace which was bestowed upon me, was not in vain; but I labored more abundantly than they all: yet not I, but the grace of God which was with me.

Rom. 12, 3 (not to think of himself more highly than he ought to think; but to think soberly); v. 10 (in honor preferring one another); James 4, 6.

NOTES AND HINTS.

Q. 1. The sixth commandment forbids all sins against the *life*, the seventh, against the *body*, the eighth, against the *property*, the ninth, against the good *name* or *honor*, of our neighbor. The third and ninth commandments are directed against the sins of the *tongue*,—the one prohibiting the abuse of the name of *God*, the other the abuse of the name of our *neighbor*.

Q. 5. All that we say must be true: but we need not, and should not, say all that is true. In silence there is often more wisdom and charity than in speech. The power of silence is an important element in true self-government.

LI. The Tenth Commandment.

1. *What is the tenth commandment?*

Thou shalt not covet thy neighbor's house, thou shalt not covet thy neighbor's wife, nor his man-servant, nor his maid-servant, nor his ox, nor his ass, nor any thing that *is* thy neighbor's.

Ex. 20, 17.—Deut. 5, 21.

2. *How does this commandment differ from the preceding commandments of the second table?*

By tracing sin to its root, the evil desires and passions of the heart, from which all evil words and deeds proceed.

* Prov. 4, 23. Keep thy heart with all diligence; for out of it are the issues of life.
James 1, 14. 15. Every man is tempted, when he is drawn away of his own lust, and enticed. Then when lust hath conceived, it bringeth forth sin: and sin, when it is finished, bringeth forth death.
Matt. 15, 19. 20. Out of the heart proceed evil thoughts [tenth commandment], murders [sixth commandment], adulteries, fornications [seventh commandment], thefts [eighth commandment], false witness, blasphemies [ninth commandment]: these are the things which defile a man.

3. *What does God forbid in this commandment?*

All envy and selfish desires after any thing that is our neighbor's.

* Gal. 5, 24. They that are Christ's have crucified the flesh with the affections [passions] and lusts.
· Col. 3, 5. Mortify... inordinate affection, evil concupiscence and covetousness, which is idolatry.
Matt. 5, 28; Rom. 7, 7; 13, 14; 1 Pet. 2, 11.

4. *What is required in this commandment?*

That we love our neighbor from the heart, wish him every blessing, and promote his temporal and eternal welfare.

* Rom. 15, 2. Let every one of us please his neighbor for his good to edification.
1 Cor. 13, 5. Charity seeketh not her own, is not easily provoked, thinketh no evil.
1 Cor. 10, 24. Let no man seek his own, but every man another's wealth [good].
Phil. 2, 4. Look not every man on his own things, but every man also on the things of others.
Comp. 1 Cor. 9, 19 (I made myself servant unto all, that I might gain the more); 10, 33 (not seeking mine own profit, but the profit of many [literally, *the* many, *i.e.* all], that they may be saved).

5. *What is the sum of all commandments?*

To love God above all things, and our neighbor as ourselves.

6. *Are you able of yourself to keep these commandments?*

No; but only by the grace of God, and the power of the Holy Spirit, who makes me perfect in every good work.

* 1 Cor. 15, 10. By the grace of God I am what I am.
2 Cor. 3, 5. Not that we are sufficient of ourselves; . . . but our sufficiency is of God.
Phil. 2, 13. It is God which worketh in you both to will and to do of his good pleasure.
Rom. 8, 3. 4. What the law could not do, in that it was weak through the flesh, God sending his own Son in the likeness of sinful flesh, and for sin, condemned sin in the flesh: that the righteousness of the law might be fulfilled in us, who walk not after the flesh, but after the Spirit.
2 Cor. 5, 17. If any man be in Christ, he is a new creature.
* Heb. 13, 20. 21. The God of peace . . . make you perfect in every good work to do his will, working in you that which is well pleasing in his sight, through Jesus Chri-

1 John 5, 3. This is the love of God, that we keep his commandments: and his commandments are not grievous [heavy, burdensome; *i.e.* they are made easy and delightful to the *believer* by the grace of God enabling him to keep them].

Matt. 11, 30. My yoke is easy, and my burden is light.

7. *Is full perfection attainable in this life?*

No; but we should constantly strive after it, and press on toward the mark, for the prize of the high calling of God in Christ Jesus.

* 1 John 1, 8. If we say we have no sin, we deceive ourselves, and the truth is not in us.

James 3, 2. In many things we offend all.

Ps. 19, 12. Who can understand his errors? Cleanse thou me from secret faults.

Phil. 3, 12-14. Not as though I had already attained [won, viz. the prize, v. 14], either were already perfect: but I follow after [press onward], if that I may apprehend that for which also I am apprehended of Christ Jesus. Brethren, I count not myself to have apprehended: but this one thing I do, forgetting those things which are behind, and reaching forth unto those things that are before, I press toward the mark for the prize of the high [heavenly] calling of God in Christ Jesus. [The image of a runner in a foot-race.]

1 Cor. 9, 24. So run that ye may obtain [the prize].

* Heb. 6, 1. Let us go on unto perfection.

8. *To whom should you look as the great model of perfection?*

We should always look unto Jesus, the author and finisher of our faith, and follow his example.

* Heb. 12, 1. 2. Let us run with patience the race that is set before us; looking unto Jesus, the author and finisher of our faith.

1 Pet. 2, 21. Christ suffered for us, leaving us an example, that ye should follow his steps.

Comp. John 12, 26 (let him follow me); 13, 15 (I have given you an example); Matt. 11, 29 (learn of me); 1 John 2, 6 (to walk, even as Christ walked); Phil. 2, 5.

THE TENTH COMMANDMENT.

NOTES AND HINTS.

Q. 1. The Roman Church in order to restore the number ten, divides the tenth commandment, making the words: "Thou shalt not covet thy neighbor's house," the ninth, and the remaining words: "Thou shalt not covet thy neighbor's wife," etc., the tenth commandment. This division is occasioned by the unwarranted omission of the second commandment. But one error falls with the other. Besides the intrinsic evidence which shows the commandment against covetousness to be an indivisible unit, a comparison of Exod. 20, 17 with Deut. 5, 21 settles the dispute in favor of the Protestant division. For in Deut. 5, 21 (as also Exod. 20, 17 in the Greek translation of the Seventy) the order is transposed, and the neighbor's wife put before the neighbor's house. This would make what is the ninth commandment in Exodus to be the tenth commandment in Deuteronomy, if the Roman view were correct. St. Paul, moreover, in enumerating the commandments of the second table, Rom. 13, 9 (comp. also 7, 7), alludes to the tenth with the words: "Thou shalt not covet," without intimating any such division. The Roman Catechism indirectly refutes its own division by treating the ninth and tenth commandments under one head (while all others are treated separately), and by expressly admitting: "We have united these two commandments, because their object is the same, and the manner of treating them should be the same."

Q. 2. Selfishness is the root of all sin, and the very opposite of love. As love is the fulfilment of all commandments, so selfishness is the violation of all commandments. The tenth and last commandment goes beyond the outward transgression by word and deed, to the secret springs of sin, and condemns it in its incipient state. It teaches that all outward observances and obedience to the letter of the law are not sufficient in themselves, but must proceed from a pure heart converted to God. It shuts up the source of all transgression, as the first commandment opens the source of all obedience and holiness, namely, love to the only true and living God. Thus the law returns to the beginning, the last commandment points to the first, and the first to the last; both point to the heart, as the source of all obedience and disobedience. This shows the deep spiritual character of the law (comp. Rom. 7, 14), as more fully brought out by our Saviour in the Sermon on the Mount. The conclusion of the decalogue points beyond the Old Testament to the New Covenant of the gospel, where God would write the law on the tables of the new, regenerate heart: comp. Jer. 31, 31 ff; Ezek. 11, 19. 20; 36, 26, 27.

Q. 3. *House* is to be taken in a general sense for all that is connected with, or belongs to, our neighbor; *wife, man-servant, maid-servant, ox, ass*, are the specifications. But in Deut. 5, 21, as also in the Greek version of Exod. 20, 17, the *wife* precedes the *house.*

Q. 4. In looking back to the second table as a whole, we see that it prohibits, in beautiful gradation, all injury to our neighbor: (1) in DEED, and that (a) in regard to his *person* (sixth commandment), (b) to his *wife* (seventh commandment), (c) to his *property* (eight commandment); (2) in WORD, by injuring his good name (ninth commandment); (3) in THOUGHT and DESIRE (tenth commandment). By prohibiting these sins, the law enjoins at the same time the opposite virtues, or love to our neighbor in *deed, word,* and *thought.* The negative or prohibitory form of the commandments of the second table points to the depravity of the human heart, which is ever ready and inclined to do what the law forbids; and thus the law, with its repeated prohibitions, "Thou shalt not do this or that," awakens and keeps alive the knowledge of sin, and leads to Christ, the Lamb of God, which taketh away the sin of the world. Christ, then, is the beginning, the middle, and the end of Christian life: Christ is all in all.

Q. 7. If the Bible nevertheless in other passages ascribes to the Christians a certain perfection (1 Cor. 2, 6; 14, 20; Eph. 4, 13; Phil. 3, 15; Heb. 5, 14; James 1, 4), we must distinguish between different *kinds* and *degrees* of perfection. There is a perfection of knowledge, and a perfection of practice, a perfection of principle and essence, and a perfection of outward manifestation, a perfection of the beginning and a perfection of the end; there is an infancy in Christ, a youth in Christ, and a full manhood in Christ.

LII. Concluding Questions.

1. *What have you now been taught?*

I have been taught how to pray, what to believe, and how to live.

2. *How should you pray?*

I should pray without ceasing to our heavenly Father, in the name of Jesus Christ our Saviour.

3. *What is the sum of the Christian faith?*

The revelation of the infinite power, wisdom, and love of God in the creation, redemption, and sanctification of the world.

4. *What is the sum of the Christian life?*

To love God above all things, and our neighbor as ourselves.

5. *What is your unerring guide in faith and practice?*

No human wisdom, which passeth away, but the word of God, which abideth forever.

6. *What is your highest aim?*

The holy and blessed communion with God the Father, the Son, and the Holy Ghost, one God, blessed forever.

7. *What is your greatest good and comfort in life or in death?*

That Christ is mine, and I am his, in body and in soul, in life and in death, now and forever. Amen.

My blessed Saviour, Lord Divine,
I am Thine own, and Thou art mine.
I am Thine own: for Thou didst give
Thy precious life, that I might live.
And Thou art mine: with all my heart
I cleave to thee, my chosen part.
How dearly didst Thou purchase me!
Oh, let me never part from Thee!

The Apostolic Benediction.

THE GRACE OF THE LORD JESUS CHRIST, AND THE LOVE OF GOD, AND THE COMMUNION OF THE HOLY GHOST, BE WITH YOU ALL. AMEN.

THE END.

www.ingramcontent.com/pod-product-compliance
Lightning Source LLC
Chambersburg PA
CBHW031451160426
43195CB00010BB/939